2nd International Workshop on Web as Corpus 2006

Held at EACL 2006

Trento, Italy
3 April 2006

ISBN: 978-1-61738-484-4

Printed from e-media with permission by:

Curran Associates, Inc.
57 Morehouse Lane
Red Hook, NY 12571
www.proceedings.com

Some format issues inherent in the e-media version may also appear in this print version.

Printed by Curran Associates, Inc. (2010)

Association for Computational Linguistics
209 N. Eighth Street
Stroudsburg, Pennsylvania 18360

Phone: 1-570-476-8006
Fax: 1-570-476-0860

acl@aclweb.org

WAC2: Programme

9.00-9.30	Marco Baroni and Adam Kilgarriff *Introduction*
9.30-10.00	András Kornai, Péter Halácsy, Viktor Nagy, Csaba Oravecz, Viktor Trón and Dániel Varga *Web-based frequency dictionaries for medium density languages*
10.00-10.30	Mike Cafarella and Oren Etzioni *BE: a search engine for NLP research*
	Break
11.00-11.30	Masatsugu Tonoike, Mitsuhiro Kida, Toshihiro Takagi, Yasuhiro Sasaki, Takehito Utsuro and Satoshi Sato *A comparative study on compositional translation estimation using a domain/topic-specific corpus collected from the web*
11.30-12.00	Gemma Boleda, Stefan Bott, Rodrigo Meza, Carlos Castillo, Toni Badia and Vicente López *CUCWeb: a Catalan corpus built from the web*
12.00-12.30	Paul Rayson, James Walkerdine, William H. Fletcher and Adam Kilgarriff *Annotated web as corpus*
	Lunch
2.30-3.00	Arno Scharl and Albert Weichselbraun *Web coverage of the 2004 US presidential election*
3.00-3.30	Cédrick Fairon *Corporator: A tool for creating RSS-based specialized corpora*
3.30-4.00	**Demos, part 1**
	Break
4.30-4.50	**Demos, part 2**
4.50-5.20	Davide Fossati, Gabriele Ghidoni, Barbara Di Eugenio, Isabel Cruz, Huiyong Xiao and Rajen Subba *The problem of ontology alignment on the web: a first report*
5.20-5.50	Kie Zuraw *Using the web as a phonological corpus: a case study from Tagalog*
5.50-6.00	*Organization, next meeting, closing*
Reserve paper	Rüdiger Gleim, Alexander Mehler and Matthias Dehmer *Web corpus mining by instance of Wikipedia*

Programme Committee

Toni Badia
Marco Baroni (co-chair)
Silvia Bernardini
Massimiliano Ciaramita
Barbara Di Eugenio
Roger Evans
Stefan Evert
William Fletcher
Rüdiger Gleim
Gregory Grefenstette
Péter Halácsy
Frank Keller
Adam Kilgarriff (co-chair)
Rob Koeling
Mirella Lapata
Anke Lüdeling
Alexander Mehler
Drago Radev
Philip Resnik
German Rigau
Serge Sharoff
David Weir

Preface

What is the role of a workshop series on web as corpus?

We argue, first, that attention to the web is critical to the health of non-corporate NLP, since the academic community runs the risk of being sidelined by corporate NLP if it does not address the issues involved in using very-large-scale web resources; second, that text type comes to the fore when we study the web, and the workshops provide a venue for nurturing this under-explored dimension of language; and thirdly that the WWW community is an important academic neighbour for CL, and the workshops will contribute to contact between CL and WWW.

High-performance NLP needs web-scale resources

The most talked-about presentation of the ACL 2005 was Franz-Josef Och's, in which he presented statistical MT results based on a 200 billion word English corpus. His results led the field. He was in a privileged position to have access to a corpus of that size. He works at Google.

With enormous data, you get better results. (See e.g. Banko and Brill 2001.) It seems to us there are two possible responses for the academic NLP community. The first is to accept defeat: "we will never have resources on the scale Google has, so we should accept that our systems will not really compete, that they will be proofs-of-concept or deal with niche problems, but will be out of the mainstream of high-performance HLT system development." The second is to say: we too need to make resources on this scale available, and they should be available to researchers in universities as well as behind corporate firewalls: and we can do it, because resources of the right scale are available, for free, on the web. We shall of course have to acquire new expertise along the way – at, *inter alia*, WAC workshops.

Text type

The most interesting question that the use of web corpora raises is text type. (We use 'text type' as a cover-all term to include domain, genre, style etc.) The first question about web corpora from an outsider is usually "how do you know that your web corpus is representative?" to which the fitting response is "how do you know whether any corpus is representative (of what?)". These questions will only receive satisfactory answers when we have a fuller account of how to identify and distinguish different kinds of text.

While text type is not centre-stage in this volume, we suspect it will be prominent in discussions at the workshop and will be the focus of papers in future workshops.

The WWW community: links, web-as-graph, and linguistics

One of CL's academic neighbours is the WWW community (as represented by, eg, the WWW conference series). Many of their key questions concern the nature of the web, viewing it as a large set of domains, or as a graph, or as a bag of bags of words. The web is substantially a linguistic object, and there is potential for these views of the web contributing to our linguistic understanding. For example, the graph structure of the web has been used to identify highly connected areas which are "web communities". How does that graph-theoretical connectedness relate to the linguistic properties one would associate with a discourse community? To date the links between the communities have been not been strong. (Few WWW papers are referenced in CL papers, and vice versa.) The workshops will provide a venue where WWW and CL interests intersect.

Recent work by co-chairs and colleagues

At risk of abusing chairs' privilege, we briefly mention two pieces of our own work. In the first we have created web corpora of over 1 billion words for German and Italian. The text has been de-duplicated, passed through a range of filters, part-of-speech tagged, lemmatized, and loaded into a web-accessible corpus query tool supporting a wide range of linguists' queries. It offers one model of how to use the web as a corpus. The corpora will be demonstrated in the main EACL conference (Baroni and Kilgarriff 2006).

In the second, WebBootCaT (work with Jan Pomikalek and Pavel Rychlý of Masaryk University, Brno), we have prepared a version of the BootCaT tools (Baroni and Bernardini 2004) as a web service. Users fill in a web form with the target language and some "seed terms" to specify the domain of the target corpus, and press the "Build Corpus" button. A corpus is built. Thus, people without any programming or software-installation skills can create corpora to their own specification. The system will be demonstrated in the "demos" session of the workshop.

The workshop series to date

This is the second international workshop, the first being held in July 2005 in Birmingham, UK (in association with Corpus Linguistics 2005). There was an earlier Italian event in Forlì, in January 2005. All three have attracted high levels of interest. The papers in this volume were selected following a highly competitive review process, and we would like to thank all those who submitted, all those on the programme committee who contributed to the review process, and the additional reviewers who helped us to get through the large number of submissions. Special thanks to Stefan Evert for help with assembling the proceedings. (Cafarella and Etzioni have an abstract rather than a full paper to avoid duplicate publication: we felt their presentation would make an important contribution to the workshop, which was a distinct issue to them not having a new text available.)

We are confident that there will be much of interest for anyone engaged with NLP and the web.

References

Banko, M. and E. Brill. 2001. "Mitigating the Paucity-of-Data Problem: Exploring the Effect of Training Corpus Size on Classifier Performance for Natural Language Processing." In Proc. Human Language Technology Conference (HLT 2001)

Baroni, M and S. Bernardini 2004. BootCaT: Bootstrapping corpora and terms from the web. Proc. LREC 2004, Lisbon: ELDA. 1313-1316.

Baroni, M. and A. Kilgarriff 2006. "Large linguistically-processed web corpora for multiple languages." Proc EACL, Trento, Italy.

Màrquez, L. and D. Klein 2006. Announcement and Call for Papers for the Tenth Conference on Computational Natural Language Learning. http://www.cnts.ua.ac.be/conll/cfp.html

Och, F-J. 2005. "Statistical Machine Translation: The Fabulous Present and Future" Invited talk at ACL Workshop on Building and Using Parallel Texts, Ann Arbor.

Adam Kilgarriff and Marco Baroni, February 2006

Table of Contents

The conference, the workshop and the tutorials are sponsored by:

Center for the Evaluation of Language and Communication Technologies

Celct
c/o BIC, Via dei Solteri, 38
38100 Trento, Italy
http://www.celct.it

Xerox Research Centre Europe
6 Chemin de Maupertuis
38240 Meylan, France
http://www.xrce.xerox.com

CELI s.r.l.
Corso Moncalieri, 21
10131 Torino, Italy
http://www.celi.it

Thales
45 rue de Villiers
92526 Neuilly-sur-Seine Cedex, France
http://www.thalesgroup.com

EACL-2006 is supported by

Trentino S.p.a. and Metalsistem Group

Web-based frequency dictionaries for medium density languages

András Kornai
MetaCarta Inc.
350 Massachusetts Avenue
Cambridge MA 02139
andras@kornai.com

Péter Halácsy
Media Research and Education Center
Stoczek u. 2
H-1111 Budapest
halacsy@mokk.bme.hu

Viktor Nagy
Institute of Linguistics
Benczúr u 33
H-1399 Budapest
nagyv@nytud.hu

Csaba Oravecz
Institute of Linguistics
Benczúr u 33
H-1399 Budapest
oravecz@nytud.hu

Viktor Trón
U of Edinburgh
2 Buccleuch Place
EH8 9LW Edinburgh
v.tron@ed.ac.uk

Dániel Varga
Media Research and Education Center
Stoczek u. 2
H-1111 Budapest
daniel@mokk.bme.hu

Abstract

Frequency dictionaries play an important role both in psycholinguistic experiment design and in language technology. The paper describes a new, freely available, web-based frequency dictionary of Hungarian that is being used for both purposes, and the language-independent techniques used for creating it.

0 Introduction

In theoretical linguistics introspective grammaticality judgments are often seen as having methodological primacy over conclusions based on what is empirically found in corpora. No doubt the main reason for this is that linguistics often studies phenomena that are not well exemplified in data. For example, in the entire corpus of written English there seems to be only one attested example, not coming from semantics papers, of Bach-Peters sentences, yet the grammaticality (and the preferred reading) of these constructions seems beyond reproach. But from the point of view of the theoretician who claims that quantifier meanings can be computed by repeat substitution, even this one example is one too many, since no such theory can account for the clearly relevant (though barely attested) facts.

In this paper we argue that ordinary corpus size has grown to the point that in some areas of theoretical linguistics, in particular for issues of inflectional morphology, the dichotomy between introspective judgments and empirical observations need no longer be maintained: in this area at least, it is now nearly possible to make the leap from zero observed frequency to zero theoretical probability i.e. ungrammaticality. In many other areas, most notably syntax, this is still untrue, and here we argue that facts of derivational morphology are not yet entirely within the reach of empirical methods. Both for inflectional and derivational morphology we base our conclusions on recent work with a gigaword web-based corpus of Hungarian (Halácsy et al 2004) which goes some way towards fulfilling the goals of the WaCky project (`http://wacky.sslmit.unibo.it`, see also Lüdeling et al 2005) inasmuch as the infrastructure used in creating it is applicable to other medium-density languages as well. Section 1 describes the creation of the WFDH Web-based Frequency Dictionary of Hungarian from the raw corpus. The critical disambiguation step required for lemmatization is discussed in Section 2, and the theoretical implications are presented in Section 3. The rest of this Introduction is devoted to some terminological clarification and the presentation of the elementary probabilistic model used for psycholinguistic experiment design.

0.1 The range of data

Here we will distinguish three kinds of corpora: *small-*, *medium-*, and *large-range*, based on the internal coherence of the component parts. A *small-range* corpus is one that is stylistically homogeneous, generally the work of a single author. The largest corpora that we could consider small-range are thus the oeuvres of the most prolific writers, rarely above 1m, and never above 10m words. A *medium-range* corpus is one that remains within the confines of a few text types, even if the authorship of individual documents can be discerned e.g. by detailed study of word usage. The LDC gigaword corpora, composed almost entirely of news (journalistic prose), are from this perspective medium range. Finally, a *large-range* corpus is one that displays a variety of text types, genres, and styles that approximates that of overall language usage – the Brown corpus at 1m words has considerably larger range than e.g. the Reuters corpus at 100m words.

The fact that psycholinguistic experiments need to control for word frequency has been known at least since Thorndike (1941) and frequency effects also play a key role in grammaticization (Bybee, 2003). Since the principal source of variability in word (n-gram) frequencies is the choice of topic, we can subsume overall considerations of genre under the selection of topics, especially as the former typically dictates the latter – for example, we rarely see literary prose or poetry dealing with undersea sedimentation rates. We assume a fixed inventory of topics $T_1, T_2, \ldots, T_k$, with k on the order 10^4, similar in granularity to the Northern Light topic hierarchy (Kornai et al 2003) and reserve T_0 to topicless texts or "General Language". Assuming that these topics appear in the language with frequency $q_1, q_2, \ldots, q_k$, summing to $1 - q_0 \leq 1$, the "average" topic is expected to have frequency about $1/k$ (and clearly, q_0 is on the same order, as it is very hard to find entirely topicless texts).

As is well known, the salience of different nouns and noun phrases appearing in the same structural position is greatly impacted not just by frequency (generally, less frequent words are more memorable) but also by stylistic value. For example, taboo words are more salient than neutral words of the same overall frequency. But style is also closely associated with topic, and if we match frequency profiles across topics we are therefore controlling for genre and style as well. Presenting psycholinguistical experiments is beyond the scope of this paper: here we put the emphasis on creating the computational resource, the frequency dictionary, that allows for detail matching of frequency profiles.

Defining the range r of a corpus C simply as $\sum_j q_j$ where the sum is taken over all topics touched by documents in C, single-author corpora typically have $r < 0.1$ even for encyclopedic writers, and web corpora have $r > 0.9$. Note that r just measures the range, it does *not* measure how representative a corpus is for some language community. Here we discuss results concerning all three ranges. For small range, we use the Hungarian translation of Orwell's *1984* – 98k words including punctuation tokens, (Dimitrova et al., 1998). For mid-range, we consider four topically segregated subcorpora of the Hungarian side of our Hungarian-English parallel corpus – 34m words, (Varga et al., 2005). For large-range we use our webcorpus – 700m words, (Halácsy et al., 2004).

1 Collecting and presenting the data

Hungarian lags behind "high density" languages like English and German but is hugely ahead of minority languages that have no significant machine readable material. Varga et al (2005) estimated there to be about 500 languages that fit in the same "medium density" category, together accounting for over 55% of the world's speakers. Halacsy et al (2004) described how a set of open source tools can be exploited to rapidly clean the results of web crawls to yield high quality monolingual corpora: the main steps are summarized below.

Raw data, preprocessing The raw dataset comes from crawling the top-level domain, e.g. `.hu, .cz, .hr, .pl` etc. Pages that contain no usable text are filtered out, and all text is converted to a uniform character encoding. Identical texts are dropped by checksum comparison of page bodies (a method that can handle near-identical pages, usually automatically generated, which differ only in their headers, datelines, menus, etc.)

Stratification A spellchecker is used to stratify pages by recognition error rates. For each page we measure the proportion of unrecognized (either incorrectly spelled or out of the vocabulary of the spellchecker) words. To filter out non-Hungarian (non-Czech, non-Croatian, non-Polish, etc.) documents, the threshold is set at 40%. If we lower the threshold to 8%, we also filter out *flat* native texts that employ Latin (7-bit) characters to denote their accented (8 bit) variants (these are still quite common due to the ubiquity of US keyboards). Finally, below the 4% threshold, webpages typically contain fewer typos than average printed documents, making the results comparable to older frequency counts based on traditional (printed) materials.

Lemmatization To turn a given stratum of the corpus into a frequency dictionary, one needs to collect the wordforms into lemmas based on the same stem: we follow the usual lexicographic practice of treating inflected, but not derived, forms of a stem as belonging to the same lemma. Inflectional stems are computed by a morphological analyzer (MA), the choice between alternative morphological analyses is resolved using the output of a POS tagger (see Section 2 below). When there are several analyses that match the output of the tagger, we choose one with the least number of identified morphemes. For now, words outside the vocabulary of the MA are not lemmatized at all – this decision will be revisited once the planned extension of the MA to a morphological guesser is complete.

Topic classification Kornai et al (2003) presented a fully automated system for the classification of webpages according to topic. Combining this method with the methods described above enables the automatic creation of topic-specific frequency dictionaries and further, the creation of a per-topic frequency distribution for each lemma. This enables much finer control of word selection in psycholinguistic experiments than was hitherto possible.

1.1 How to present the data?

For Hungarian, the highest quality (4% threshold) stratum of the corpus contains 1.22m unique pages for a total of 699m tokens, already exceeding the 500m predicted in (Kilgarriff and Grefenstette, 2003). Since the web has grown considerably since the crawl (which took place in 2003), their estimate was clearly on the conservative side. Of the 699m tokens some 4.95m were outside the vocabulary of the MA (7% OOV in this mode, but less than 3% if numerals are excluded and the analysis of compounds is turned on). The remaining 649.7m tokens fall in 195k lemmas with an average 54 form types per lemma. If all stems are considered, the ratio is considerably lower, 33.6, but the average entropy of the inflectional distributions goes down only from 1.70 to 1.58 bits.

As far as the summary frequency list (which is less than a megabyte compressed) is concerned, this can be published trivially. Clearly, the availability of large-range gigaword corpora is in the best interest of all workers in language technology, and equally clearly, only open (freely downloadable) materials allow for replicability of experiments. While it is possible to exploit search engine queries for various NLP tasks (Lapata and Keller, 2004), for applications which use corpora as unsupervised training material downloadable base data is essential.

Therefore, a compiled webcorpus should contain actual texts. We believe all "cover your behind" efforts such as publishing only URLs to be fundamentally misguided. First, URLs age very rapidly: in any given year more than 10% become stale (Cho and Garcia-Molina, 2000), which makes any experiment conducted on such a basis effectively irreproducible. Second, by presenting a quality-filtered and characterset-normalized corpus the collectors actually perform a service to those who are less interested in such mundane issues. If everybody has to start their work from the ground up, many projects will exhaust their funding resources and allotted time before anything interesting could be done with the data. In contrast, the Free and Open Source Software (FOSS) model actively encourages researchers to reuse data.

In this regard, it is worth mentioning that during the crawls we always respected `robots.txt` and in the two years since the publication of the gigaword Hungarian web corpus, there has not been a single request by copyright holders to remove material. We do not advocate piracy: to the contrary, it is our intended policy to comply with removal requests from copyright holders, analogous to Google cache removal requests. Finally, even with copyright material, there are easy methods for preserving interesting linguistic data (say unigram and bigram models) without violating the interests of businesses involved in selling the running texts. [1]

2 The disambiguation of morphological analyses

In any morphologically complex language, the MA component will often return more than one possible analysis. In order to create a lemmatized frequency dictionary it is necessary to decide which MA alternative is the correct one, and in the vast majority of cases the context provides sufficient information for this. This morphological disambiguation task is closely related to, but not identical with, part of speech (POS) tagging, a term we reserve here for finding the major parts

[1]This year, we are publishing smaller pilot corpora for Czech (10m words), Croatian (4m words), and Polish (12m words), and we feel confident in predicting that these will face as little actual opposition from copyright holders as the Hungarian Webcorpus has.

of speech (N, V, A, etc). A full tag contains both POS information and morphological annotation: in highly inflecting languages the latter can lead to tagsets of high cardinality (Tufiş et al., 2000). Hungarian is particularly challenging in this regard, both because the number of ambiguous tokens is high (reaching 50% in the Szeged Corpus according to (Csendes et al., 2004) who use a different MA), and because the ratio of tokens that are not seen during training (unseen) can be as much as four times higher than in comparable size English corpora. But if larger training corpora are available, significant disambiguation is possible: with a 1 m word training corpus (Csendes et al., 2004) the TnT (Brants, 2000) architecture can achieve 97.42% overall precision.

The ratio of ambiguous tokens is usually calculated based on alternatives offered by a morphological lexicon (either built during the training process or furnished by an external application; see below). If the lexicon offers alternative analyses, the token is taken as ambiguous irrespective of the probability of the alternatives. If an external resource is used in the form of a morphological analyzer (MA), this will almost always overgenerate, yielding false ambiguity. But even if the MA is tight, a considerable proportion of ambiguous tokens will come from legitimate but rare analyses of frequent types (Church, 1988). For example the word *nem*, can mean both 'not' and 'gender', so both `ADV` and `NOUN` are valid analyses, but the adverbial reading is about five orders of magnitude more frequent than the noun reading, (12596 vs. 4 tokens in the 1 m word manually annotated Szeged Korpusz (Csendes et al., 2004)).

Thus the difficulty of the task is better measured by the average information required for disambiguating a token. If word w is assigned the label T_i with probability $P(T_i|w)$ (estimated as $C(T_i, w)/C(w)$ from a labeled corpus) then the label entropy for a word can be calculated as $H(w) = -\sum_i P(T_i|w) \log P(T_i|w)$, and the difficulty of the labeling task as a whole is the weighted average of these entropies with respect to the frequencies of words w: $\sum_w P(w)H(w)$. As we shall see in Section 3, according to this measure the disambiguation task is not as difficult as generally assumed.

A more persistent problem is that the ratio of unseen items has very significant influence on the performance of the disambiguation system. The problem is more significant with smaller corpora: in general, if the training corpus has N tokens and the test corpus is a constant fraction of this, say $N/10$, we expect the proportion of new words to be cN^{q-1}, where q is the reciprocal of the Zipf constant (Kornai, 1999). But if the test/train ratio is not kept constant because the training corpus is limited (manual tagging is expensive), the number of tokens that are not seen during training can grow very large. Using the 1.2 m words of Szeged Corpus for training, in the 699 m word webcorpus over 4% of the non-numeric tokens will be unseen. Given that TnT performs rather dismally on unseen items (Oravecz and Dienes, 2002) it was clear from the outset that for lemmatizing the webcorpus we needed something more elaborate.

The standard solution to constrain the probabilistic tagging model for some of the unseen items is the application of MA (Hakkani-Tür et al., 2000; Hajič et al., 2001; Smith et al., 2005). Here a distinction must be made between those items that are not found in the training corpus (these we have called *unseen* tokens) and those that are not known to the MA – we call these out of vocabulary (OOV). As we shall see shortly, the key to the best tagging architecture we found was to follow different strategies in the lemmatization and morphological disambiguation of OOV and known (in-vocabulary) tokens.

The first step in tagging is the annotation of inflectional features, with lemmatization being postponed to later processing as in (Erjavec and Džeroski, 2004). This differs from the method of (Hakkani-Tür et al., 2000), where all syntactically relevant features (including the stem or lemma) of word forms are determined in one pass. In our experience, the choice of stem depends so heavily on the type of linguistic information that later processing will need that it cannot be resolved in full generality at the morphosyntactic level.

Our first model (MA-ME) is based on disambiguating the MA output in the maximum entropy (ME) framework (Ratnaparkhi, 1996). In addition to the MA output, we use ME features coding the surface form of the preceding/following word, capitalization information, and different character length suffix strings of the current word. The MA used is the open-source `hunmorph` analyzer (Trón et al., 2005) with the `morphdb.hu` Hungarian morphological resource, the ME is the OpenNLP package (Baldridge et al., 2001). The

MA-ME model achieves 97.72% correct POS tagging and morphological analysis on the test corpus (not used in training).

Maximum entropy or other discriminative Markov models (McCallum et al., 2000) suffer from the label bias problem (Lafferty et al., 2001), while generative models (most notably HMMs) need strict independence assumptions to make the task of sequential data labeling tractable. Consequently, long distance dependencies and non-independent features cannot be handled. To cope with these problems we designed a hybrid architecture, in which a trigram HMM is combined with the MA in such a way that for tokens known to the MA only the set of possible analyses are allowed as states in the HMM whereas for OOVs all states are possible. Lexical probabilities $P(w_i|t_i)$ for seen words are estimated from the training corpus, while for unseen tokens they are provided by the the above MA-ME model. This yields a trigram HMM where emission probabilities are estimated by a weighted MA, hence the model is called WMA-T3. This improves the score to 97.93%.

Finally, it is possible to define another architecture, somewhat similar to Maximum Entropy Markov Models, (McCallum et al., 2000), using the above components. Here states are also the set of analyses the MA allows for known tokens and all analyses for OOVs, while emission probabilities are estimated by the MA-ME model. In the first pass TnT is run with default settings over the data sequence, and in the second pass the ME receives as features the TnT label of the preceding/following token as well as the one to be analyzed. This combined system (TnT-MA-ME) incorporates the benefits of all the submodules and reaches an accuracy of 98.17% on the Szeged Corpus. The results are summarized in Table 1.

model	accuracy
TnT	97.42
MA+ME	97.72
WMA+T3	97.93
TnT+MA+ME	98.17

Table 1: accuracy of morphological disambiguation

We do not consider these results to be final: clearly, further enhancements are possible e.g. by a Viterbi search on alternative sentence taggings using the T3 trigram tag model or by handling OOVs on a par with known unseen words using the guesser function of our MA. But, as we discuss in more detail in Halacsy et al 2005, we are already ahead of the results published elsewhere, especially as these tend to rely on idealized MA systems that have their morphological resources extended so as to have no OOV on the test set.

3 Conclusions

Once the disambiguation of morphological analyses is under control, lemmatization itself is a mechanical task which we perform in a database framework. This has the advantage that it supports a rich set of query primitives, so that we can easily find e.g. nouns with back vowels that show stem vowel elision and have approximately the same frequency as the stem *orvos* 'doctor'. Such a database has obvious applications both in psycholinguistic experiments (which was one of the design goals) and in settling questions of theoretical morphology. But there are always nagging doubts about the closed world assumption behind databases, famously exposed in linguistics by Chomsky's example *colorless green ideas sleep furiously:* how do we distinguish this from **green sleep colorless furiously ideas* if the observed frequency is zero for both?

Clearly, a naive empirical model that assigns zero probability to each unseen word form makes the wrong predictions. Better estimates can be achieved if unseen words which are known to be possible morphologically complex forms of seen lemmas are assigned positive probability. This can be done if the probability of a complex form is in some way predictable from the probabilities of its component parts. A simple variant of this model is the positional independence hypothesis which takes the probabilities of morphemes in separate positional classes to be independent of each other. Here we follow Antal (1961) and Kornai (1992) in establishing three positional classes in the inflectional paradigm of Hungarian nouns.

```
# Position 1 parameters
FAM                      0.0001038986
PLUR                     0.1372398793
PLUR_POSS                0.0210927964
PLUR_POSS<1>             0.0011609442
PLUR_POSS<1><PLUR>       0.0028751247
PLUR_POSS<2>             0.0004958278
PLUR_POSS<2><PLUR>       0.0000740203
PLUR_POSS<PLUR>          0.0023850120
POSS                     0.1461635946
```

POSS<1>	0.0073305415
POSS<1><PLUR>	0.0073652648
POSS<1>_FAM	0.0000092294
POSS<2>	0.0027628071
POSS<2><PLUR>	0.0003006440
POSS<2>_FAM	0.0000030591
POSS<PLUR>	0.0069613929
POSS_FAM	0.0000000001
ZERO1	0.6636759634
# Position 2 parameters	
ANP	0.0007780001
ANP<PLUR>	0.0000248301
ZERO2	0.9991971698
# Position 3 parameters	
CAS<ABL>	0.0078638013
CAS<ACC>	0.1346412632
CAS<ADE>	0.0045132704
CAS<ALL>	0.0138677701
CAS<CAU>	0.0037332025
CAS<DAT>	0.0301123636
CAS<DEL>	0.0128222999
CAS<ELA>	0.0118596792
CAS<ESS>	0.0010230505
CAS<FOR>	0.0031204983
CAS<ILL>	0.0154186683
CAS<INE>	0.0582887516
CAS<INS>	0.0406197868
CAS<SBL>	0.0386519707
CAS<SUE>	0.0357416253
CAS<TEM>	0.0013095685
CAS<TER>	0.0034032438
CAS<TRA>	0.0017860054
ZERO3	0.5812231804

Table 3: marginal probabilities in noun inflection

The innermost class is used for number and possessive, with a total of 18 choices including the zero morpheme (no possessor and singular). The second positional class is for anaphoric possessives with a total of three choices including the zero morpheme, and the third (outermost) class is for case endings with a total of 19 choices including the zero morpheme (nominative) for a total of 1026 paradigmatic forms. The parameters were obtained by downhill simplex minimization of absolute errors. The average absolute error is of the values computed by the independece hypothesis from the observed values is 0.000099 (mean squared error is $9.18 \cdot 10^{-7}$), including the 209 paradigmatic slots for which no forms were found in the webcorpus at all (but the independence model will assign positive probability to any of them as the product of the component probabilities). When checking the independence hypothesis with Φ statistics in the webcorpus for every nominal inflectional morpheme pair the members of which are from different dimensions, the Φ coefficient remained less than 0.1 for each pair but 3. For these 3 the coefficient is under 0.2 (which means that the shared variance of these pairs is between 1% and 2%) so we have no reason to discard the independence hypothesis. If we run the same test on the 150 million words Hungarian National Corpus, which was analyzed and tagged by different tools, we also get the same result (Nagy, 2005).

It is very easy to construct low probability combinations using this model. Taking a less frequent possessive ending such as the 2nd singular posessor familiar plural *-odék*, the anaphoric plural *-éi*, and a rarer case ending such as the formalis *-ként* we obtain combinations such as *barátodékéiként* "as the objects owned by your friends' company". The model predicts we need a corpus with about $4.2 \cdot 10^{12}$ noun tokens to see this suffix combination (not necessarily with the stem *barát* "friend") or about ten trillion tokens. While the current corpus falls short by four orders of magnitude, this is about the contribution of the anaphoric plural (which we expect to see only once in about 40k noun tokens) so for any two of the three position classes combined the prediction that valid inflectional combinations will actually be attested is already testable.

Using the fitted distribution of the position classes, the entropy of the nominal paradigm is computed simply as the sum of the class entropies, 1.554 + 0.0096 + 2.325 or 3.888 bits. Since the nominal paradigm is considerably more complex than the verbal paradigm (which has a total of 52 forms) or the infinitival paradigm (7 forms), this value can serve as an upper bound on the inflectional entropy of Hungarian. In Table 3 we present the actual values, computed on a variety of frequency dictionaries. The smallest of these is based on a single text, the Hungarian translation of Orwell's *1984*. The mid-range corpora used in this comparison are segregated in broad topics: law (EU laws and regulations), literature, movie subtitles, and software manuals: all were collected from the web as part of building a bilingual English-Hungarian corpus. Finally, the large-range is the full webcorpus at the best (4% reject) quality stratum.

	1984	law	literature	subtitles	software	webcorpus
token	98292	2310742	7971157	2667420	839339	69926550
type	20343	110040	431615	188131	81729	2083023
OOV token	3141	266368	335660	181292	140551	4951743
OOV type	1132	39467	87574	50078	45799	994890
lemma	10644	60602	165259	85491	58939	1189471
lemma excl. OOV	9513	21136	77686	35414	13141	194589
lemma entropy	1.14282	1.04118	1.54922	1.41374	1.14516	1.57708
lemma entropy excl. OOV	1.18071	1.17687	1.61753	1.51718	1.37559	1.69743

Table 3: inflectional entropy of Hungarian computed on a variety of frequency dictionaries

Our overall conclusion is that for many purposes a web-based corpus has significant advantages over more traditional corpora. First, it is cheap to collect. Second, it is sufficiently heterogeneous to ensure that language models based on it generalize better on new texts of arbitrary topics than models built on (balanced) manual corpora. As we have shown, automatically tagged and lemmatized webcorpora can be used to obtain large coverage stem and wordform frequency dictionaries. While there is a significant portion of OOV entries (about 3% for our current MA), in the design of psycholinguistic experiments it is generally sufficient to consider stems already known to the MA, and the variety of these (over three times the stem lexicon of the standard Hungarian frequency dictionary) enables many controlled experiments hitherto impossible.

References

László Antal. 1961. A magyar esetrendszer. *Nyelvtudományi Értekezések*, 29.

Jason Baldridge, Thomas Morton, and Gann Bierner. 2001. The opennlp maximum entropy package. *http://maxent.sourceforge.net*.

Thorsten Brants. 2000. TnT – a statistical part-of-speech tagger. In *Proceedings of the Sixth Applied Natural Language Processing Conference (ANLP-2000)*, Seattle, WA.

Joan Bybee. 2003. Mechanisms of change in grammaticization: the role of frequency. In Brian Joseph and Richard Janda, editors, *Handbook of Historical Linguistics*, pages 602–623. Blackwell.

Junghoo Cho and Hector Garcia-Molina. 2000. The evolution of the web and implications for an incremental crawler. In *VLDB '00: Proceedings of the 26th International Conference on Very Large Data Bases*, pages 200–209, San Francisco, CA, USA. Morgan Kaufmann Publishers Inc.

Kenneth Ward Church. 1988. A stochastic parts program and noun phrase parser for unrestricted text. In *Proceedings of the second conference on Applied natural language processing*, pages 136–143, Morristown, NJ, USA. Association for Computational Linguistics.

Dóra Csendes, János Csirik, and Tibor Gyimóthy. 2004. The Szeged Corpus: A POS tagged and syntactically annotated Hungarian natural language corpus. In Karel Pala Petr Sojka, Ivan Kopecek, editor, *Text, Speech and Dialogue: 7th International Conference, TSD*, pages 41–47.

Ludmila Dimitrova, Tomaz Erjavec, Nancy Ide, Heiki Jaan Kaalep, Vladimir Petkevic, and Dan Tufiş. 1998. Multext-east: Parallel and comparable corpora and lexicons for six central and eastern european languages. In Christian Boitet and Pete Whitelock, editors, *Proceedings of the Thirty-Sixth Annual Meeting of the Association for Computational Linguistics and Seventeenth International Conference on Computational Linguistics*, pages 315–319, San Francisco, California. Morgan Kaufmann Publishers.

Tomaž Erjavec and Sašo Džeroski. 2004. Machine learning of morphosyntactic structure: Lemmatizing unknown Slovene words. *Applied Artificial Intelligence*, 18(1):17–41.

Jan Hajič, Pavel Krbec, Karel Oliva, Pavel Květoň, and Vladimír Petkevič. 2001. Serial combination of rules and statistics: A case study in Czech tagging. In *Proceedings of the 39th Association of Computational Linguistics Conference*, pages 260–267, Toulouse, France.

Dilek Z. Hakkani-Tür, Kemal Oflazer, and Gökhan Tür. 2000. Statistical morphological disambiguation for agglutinative languages. In *Proceedings of the 18th conference on Computational linguistics*, pages 285–291, Morristown, NJ, USA. Association for Computational Linguistics.

Péter Halácsy, András Kornai, László Németh, András Rung, István Szakadát, and Viktor Trón. 2004. Creating open language resources for Hungarian. In *Proceedings of Language Resources and Evaluation Conference (LREC04)*. European Language Resources Association.

Péter Halácsy, András Kornai, and Dániel Varga. 2005. Morfológiai egyértelműsítés maximum entrópia módszerrel (morphological disambiguation with the maxent method). In *Proc. 3rd Hungarian Computational Linguistics Conf.* Szegedi Tudományegyetem.

Adam Kilgarriff and Gregory Grefenstette. 2003. Introduction to the special issue on the web as corpus. *Computational Linguistics*, 29(3):333–348.

András Kornai, Marc Krellenstein, Michael Mulligan, David Twomey, Fruzsina Veress, and Alec Wysoker. 2003. Classifying the hungarian web. In A. Copestake and J. Hajic, editors, *Proc. EACL*, pages 203–210.

András Kornai. 1992. Frequency in morphology. In I. Kenesei, editor, *Approaches to Hungarian*, volume IV, pages 246–268.

András Kornai. 1999. Zipf's law outside the middle range. In J. Rogers, editor, *Proc. Sixth Meeting on Mathematics of Language*, pages 347–356. University of Central Florida.

John Lafferty, Andrew McCallum, and Fernando Pereira. 2001. Conditional random fields: Probabilistic models for segmenting and labeling sequence data. In *Proceedings of the 18th International Conference on Machine Learning*, pages 282–289. Morgan Kaufmann, San Francisco, CA.

Mirella Lapata and Frank Keller. 2004. The web as a baseline: Evaluating the performance of unsupervised web-based models for a range of NLP tasks. In Daniel Marcu Susan Dumais and Salim Roukos, editors, *HLT-NAACL 2004: Main Proceedings*, pages 121–128, Boston, Massachusetts, USA, May 2 - May 7. Association for Computational Linguistics.

Anke Luedeling, Stefan Evert, and Marco Baroni. 2005. Using web data for linguistic purposes. In Marianne Hundt, Caroline Biewer, and Nadjia Nesselhauf, editors, *Corpus linguistics and the Web*. Rodopi.

Andrew McCallum, Dayne Freitag, and Fernando Pereira. 2000. Maximum entropy Markov models for information extraction and segmentation. In *Proceedings of the 17th International Conference on Machine Learning*, pages 591–598. Morgan Kaufmann, San Francisco, CA.

Viktor Nagy. 2005. A magyar főnévi inflexió statisztikai modellje (statistical model of nominal inflection in hungarian. In *Proc. Kodolányi-ELTE Conf.*

Csaba Oravecz and Péter Dienes. 2002. Efficient stochastic part-of-speech tagging for Hungarian. In *Proceedings of the Third International Conference on Language Resources and Evaluation (LREC2002)*, pages 710–717.

Adwait Ratnaparkhi. 1996. A maximum entropy model for part-of-speech tagging. In Karel Pala Petr Sojka, Ivan Kopecek, editor, *Proceedings of the Conference on Empirical Methods in Natural Language Processing*, pages 133–142, University of Pennsylvania.

Noah A. Smith, David A. Smith, and Roy W. Tromble. 2005. Context-based morphological disambiguation with random fields. In *Proceedings of the Conference on Human Language Technology and Empirical Methods in Natural Language Processing*, Vancouver.

Edward L. Thorndike. 1941. *The Teaching of English Suffixes*. Teachers College, Columbia University.

Viktor Trón, György Gyepesi, Péter Halácsy, András Kornai, László Németh, and Dániel Varga. 2005. Hunmorph: open source word analysis. In *Proceeding of the ACL 2005 Workshop on Software*.

Dan Tufiş, Péter Dienes, Csaba Oravecz, and Tamás Váradi. 2000. Principled hidden tagset design for tiered tagging of Hungarian. In *Proceedings of the Second International Conference on Language Resources and Evaluation*.

Dániel Varga, László Németh, Péter Halácsy, András Kornai, Viktor Trón, and Viktor Nagy. 2005. Parallel corpora for medium density languages. In *Proceedings of the Recent Advances in Natural Language Processing 2005 Conference*, pages 590–596, Borovets. Bulgaria.

BE: A Search Engine for NLP Research

Michael J. Cafarella, Oren Etzioni
Department of Computer Science and Engineering
University of Washington
Seattle, WA 98195-2350
{mjc,etzioni}@cs.washington.edu

Many modern natural language-processing applications utilize search engines to locate large numbers of Web documents or to compute statistics over the Web corpus. Yet Web search engines are designed and optimized for simple human queries—they are not well suited to support such applications. As a result, these applications are forced to issue millions of successive queries resulting in unnecessary search engine load and in slow applications with limited scalability.

In response, we have designed the Bindings Engine (BE), which supports queries containing *typed variables* and *string-processing functions* (Cafarella and Etzioni, 2005). For example, in response to the query *"powerful* ⟨*noun*⟩*"* BE will return all the nouns in its index that immediately follow the word "powerful", sorted by frequency. (Figure 1 shows several possible BE queries.) In response to the query *"Cities such as ProperNoun(Head(*⟨*NounPhrase*⟩*))"*, BE will return a list of proper nouns likely to be city names.

president Bush <*Verb*>
cities such as *ProperNoun(Head(*<*NounPhrase*>*))*
<*NounPhrase*> is the CEO of <*NounPhrase*>

Figure 1: **Examples of queries that can be handled by BE. Queries that include typed variables and string-processing functions allow certain NLP tasks to be done very efficiently.**

BE's novel *neighborhood index* enables it to do so with $O(k)$ random disk seeks and $O(k)$ serial disk reads, where k is the number of non-variable terms in its query. A standard search engine requires $O(k + B)$ random disk seeks, where B is the number of variable "bindings" found in the corpus. Since B is typically very large, BE vastly reduces the number of random disk seeks needed to process a query. Such seeks operate very slowly and make up the bulk of query-processing time. As a result, BE can yield several orders of magnitude speedup for large-scale language-processing applications. The main cost is a modest increase in space to store the index.

To illustrate BE's capabilities, we have built an application to support interactive information extraction in response to simple user queries. For example, in response to the user query "insects", the application returns the results shown in Figure 2. The application

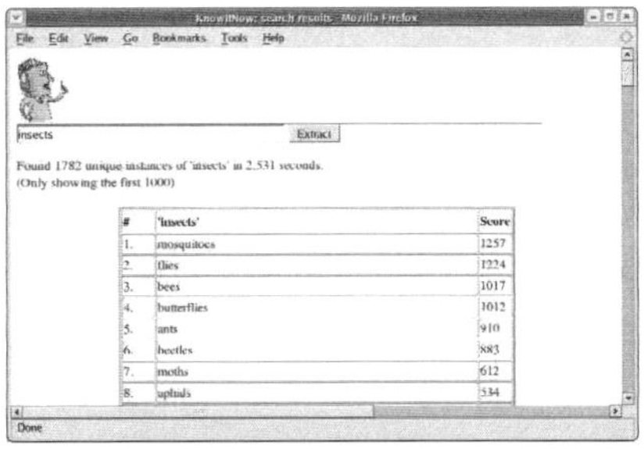

Figure 2: **Most-frequently-seen extractions for query "insects". The score for each extraction is the number of times it was retrieved over several BE extraction phrases.**

generates this list by using the query term to instantiate a set of generic extraction phrase queries such as "insects such as ⟨*NounPhrase*⟩". In effect, the application is doing a kind of query expansion to enable naive users to extract information. In an effort to find high-quality extractions, we sort the list by the hit count for each binding, summed over all the queries.

The key difference between this BE application, called KNOWITNOW, and domain-independent information extraction systems such as KNOWITALL (Etzioni et al., 2005) is that BE enables extraction at interactive speeds — the average time to expand and respond to a user query is between 1 and 45 seconds. With additional optimization, we believe we can reduce that time to 5 seconds or less. A detailed description of KNOWITNOW appears in (Cafarella et al., 2005).

References

M. Cafarella and O. Etzioni. 2005. A Search Engine for Natural Language Applications. In *Procs. of the 14th International World Wide Web Conference (WWW 2005)*.

M. Cafarella, D. Downey, S. Soderland, and O. Etzioni. 2005. Knowitnow: Fast, scalable information extraction from the web. In *Procs. of EMNLP*.

O. Etzioni, M. Cafarella, D. Downey, S. Kok, A. Popescu, T. Shaked, S. Soderland, D. Weld, and A. Yates. 2005. Unsupervised named-entity extraction from the web: An experimental study. *Artificial Intelligence*, 165(1):91–134.

A Comparative Study on Compositional Translation Estimation using a Domain/Topic-Specific Corpus collected from the Web

Masatsugu Tonoike†, Mitsuhiro Kida†, Toshihiro Takagi†, Yasuhiro Sasaki†, Takehito Utsuro††, Satoshi Sato† † †

†Graduate School of Informatics, Kyoto University
Yoshida-Honmachi, Sakyo-ku, Kyoto 606-8501, Japan

††Graduate School of Systems and Information Engineering, University of Tsukuba
1-1-1, Tennodai, Tsukuba, 305-8573, Japan

† † †Graduate School of Engineering, Nagoya University
Furo-cho, Chikusa-ku, Nagoya 464-8603, Japan

Abstract

This paper studies issues related to the compilation of a bilingual lexicon for technical terms. In the task of estimating bilingual term correspondences of technical terms, it is usually rather difficult to find an existing corpus for the domain of such technical terms. In this paper, we adopt an approach of collecting a corpus for the domain of such technical terms from the Web. As a method of translation estimation for technical terms, we employ a compositional translation estimation technique. This paper focuses on quantitatively comparing variations of the components in the scoring functions of compositional translation estimation. Through experimental evaluation, we show that the domain/topic-specific corpus contributes toward improving the performance of the compositional translation estimation.

1 Introduction

This paper studies issues related to the compilation of a bilingual lexicon for technical terms. Thus far, several techniques of estimating bilingual term correspondences from a parallel/comparable corpus have been studied (Matsumoto and Utsuro, 2000). For example, in the case of estimation from comparable corpora, (Fung and Yee, 1998; Rapp, 1999) proposed standard techniques of estimating bilingual term correspondences from comparable corpora. In their techniques, contextual similarity between a source language term and its translation candidate is measured across the languages, and all the translation candidates are re-ranked according to their contextual similarities. However, there are limited number of parallel/comparable corpora that are available for the purpose of estimating bilingual term correspondences. Therefore, even if one wants to apply those existing techniques to the task of estimating bilingual term correspondences of technical terms, it is usually rather difficult to find an existing corpus for the domain of such technical terms.

On the other hand, compositional translation estimation techniques that use a monolingual corpus (Fujii and Ishikawa, 2001; Tanaka and Baldwin, 2003) are more practical. It is because collecting a monolingual corpus is less expensive than collecting a parallel/comparable corpus. Translation candidates of a term can be compositionally generated by concatenating the translation of the constituents of the term. Here, the generated translation candidates are validated using the domain/topic-specific corpus.

In order to assess the applicability of the compositional translation estimation technique, we randomly pick up 667 Japanese and English technical term translation pairs of 10 domains from existing technical term bilingual lexicons. We then manually examine their compositionality, and find out that 88% of them are actually compositional, which is a very encouraging result.

But still, it is expensive to collect a domain/topic-specific corpus. Here, we adopt an approach of using the Web, since documents of various domains/topics are available on the Web. When validating translation candidates using the Web, roughly speaking, there exist the following two approaches. In the first approach, translation candidates are validated through the search engine (Cao and Li, 2002). In the second approach, a domain/topic-specific corpus is collected from the Web in advance and fixed

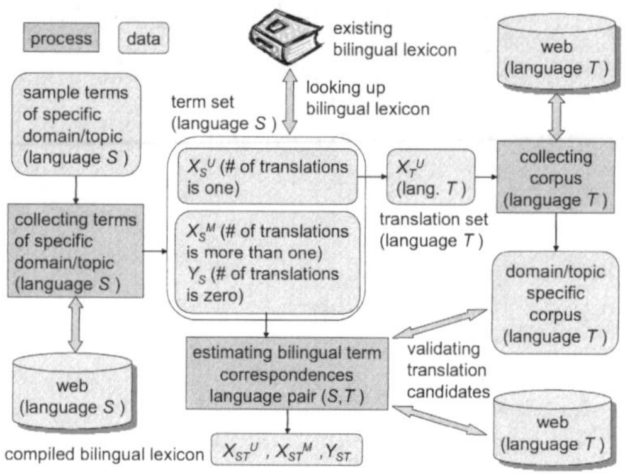

Figure 1: Compilation of a Domain/Topic-Specific Bilingual Lexicon using the Web

before translation estimation, then generated translation candidates are validated against the domain/topic-specific corpus (Tonoike et al., 2005). The first approach is preferable in terms of coverage, while the second is preferable in terms of computational efficiency. This paper mainly focuses on quantitatively comparing the two approaches in terms of coverage and precision of compositional translation estimation.

More specifically, in compositional translation estimation, we decompose the scoring function of a translation candidate into two components: bilingual lexicon score and corpus score. In this paper, we examine variants for those components and define 9 types of scoring functions in total. Regarding the above mentioned two approaches to validating translation candidates using the Web, the experimental result shows that the second approach outperforms the first when the correct translation does exist in the corpus. Furthermore, we examine the methods that combine two scoring functions based on their agreement. The experimental result shows that it is quite possible to achieve precision much higher than those of single scoring functions.

2 Overall framework

The overall framework of compiling a bilingual lexicon from the Web is illustrated as in Figure 1. Suppose that we have sample terms of a specific domain/topic, then the technical terms that are to be listed as the headwords of a bilingual lexicon are collected from the Web by the related term collection method of (Sato and Sasaki, 2003). These collected technical terms can be divided into three subsets depending on the number of translation candidates present in an existing bilingual lexicon, i.e., the subset X_S^U of terms for which the number of translations in the existing bilingual lexicon is one, the subset X_S^M of terms for which the number of translations is more than one, and the subset Y_S of terms that are not found in the existing bilingual lexicon (henceforth, the union $X_S^U \cup X_S^M$ will be denoted as X_S). Here, the translation estimation task here is to estimate translations for the terms of the subsets X_S^M and Y_S. A new bilingual lexicon is compiled from the result of the translation estimation for the terms of the subsets X_S^M and Y_S as well as the translation pairs that consist of the terms of the subset X_S^U and their translations found in the existing bilingual lexicon.

For the terms of the subset X_S^M, it is required that an appropriate translation is selected from among the translation candidates found in the existing bilingual lexicon. For example, as a translation of the Japanese technical term "レジスタ," which belongs to the *logic circuit* domain, the term "register" should be selected but not the term "regista" of the *football* domain. On the other hand, for the terms of Y_S, it is required that the translation candidates are generated and validated. In this paper, out of the above two tasks, we focus on the latter of translation candidate generation and validation using the Web. As we introduced in the previous section, here we experimentally compare the two approaches to validating translation candidates. The first approach directly uses the search engine, while the second uses the domain/topic-specific corpus, which is collected in advance from the Web. Here, in the second approach, we use the term of X_S^U, which has only one translation in the existing bilingual lexicon. The set of translations of the terms of the subset X_S^U is denoted as X_T^U. Then, in the second approach, the domain/topic-specific corpus is collected from the Web using the terms of the set X_T^U.

3 Compositional Translation Estimation for Technical Terms

3.1 Overview

An example of compositional translation estimation for the Japanese technical term "応用行動分析" is illustrated in Figure 2. First, the Japanese technical term "応用行動分析" is decomposed into its constituents by consulting an existing bilingual lexicon and retrieving Japanese head-

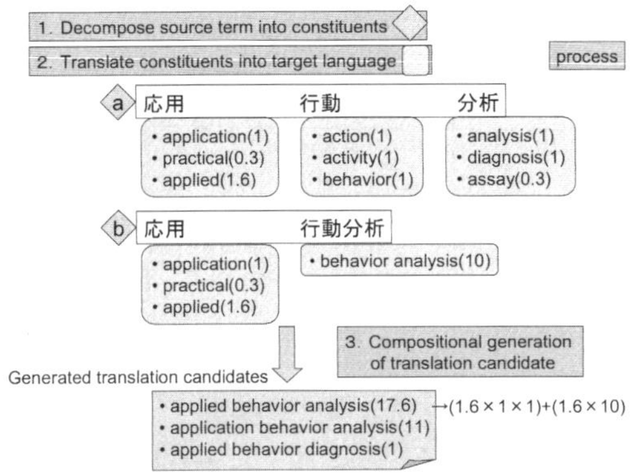

Figure 2: Compositional Translation Estimation for the Japanese Technical Term "応用行動分析"

words.[1] In this case, the result of this decomposition can be given as in the cases "a" and "b" (in Figure 2). Then, each constituent is translated into the target language. A confidence score is assigned to the translation of each constituent. Finally, translation candidates are generated by concatenating the translation of those constituents according to word ordering rules considering prepositional phrase construction.

3.2 Collecting a Domain/Topic-Specific Corpus

When collecting a domain/topic-specific corpus of the language T, for each technical term x_T^U in the set X_T^U, we collect the top 100 pages obtained from search engine queries that include the term x_T^U. Our search engine queries are designed such that documents that describe the technical term x_T^U are ranked high. For example, an online glossary is one such document. When collecting a Japanese corpus, the search engine "goo"[2] is used. The specific queries that are used in this search engine are phrases with topic-marking postpositional particles such as "x_T^U とは," "x_T^U という," "x_T^U は," and an adnominal phrase "x_T^U の," and "x_T^U."

3.3 Translation Estimation

3.3.1 Compiling Bilingual Constituents Lexicons

This section describes how to compile bilingual constituents lexicons from the translation pairs of

[1]Here, as an existing bilingual lexicon, we use Eijiro(http://www.alc.co.jp/) and bilingual constituents lexicons compiled from the translation pairs of Eijiro (details to be described in the next section).

[2]http://www.goo.ne.jp/

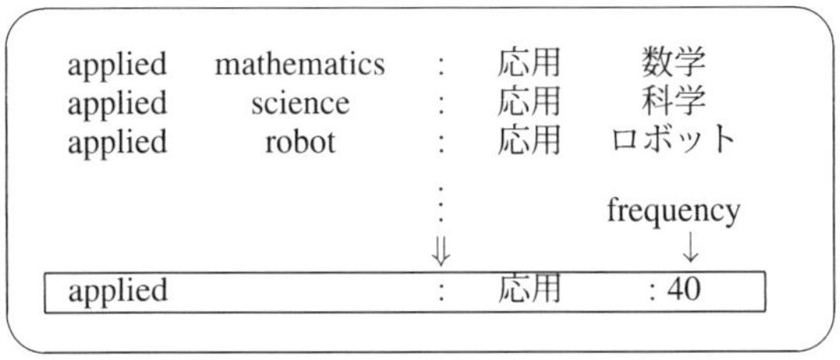

Figure 3: Example of Estimating Bilingual Constituents Translation Pair (Prefix)

the existing bilingual lexicon Eijiro. The underlying idea of augmenting the existing bilingual lexicon with bilingual constituents lexicons is illustrated in Figure 3. Suppose that the existing bilingual lexicon does not include the translation pair "applied : 応用," while it includes many compound translation pairs with the first English word "applied" and the first Japanese word "応用."[3] In such a case, we align those translation pairs and estimate a bilingual constituent translation pair which is to be collected into a bilingual constituents lexicon.

More specifically, from the existing bilingual lexicon, we first collect translation pairs whose English terms and Japanese terms consist of two constituents into another lexicon P_2. We compile the "bilingual constituents lexicon (prefix)" from the first constituents of the translation pairs in P_2 and compile the "bilingual constituents lexicon (suffix)" from their second constituents. The number of entries in each language and those of the translation pairs in these lexicons are shown in Table 1.

The result of our assessment reveals that only 48% of the 667 translation pairs mentioned in Section 1 can be compositionally generated by using Eijiro, while the rate increases up to 69% using both Eijiro and "bilingual constituents lexicons."[4]

3.3.2 Score of Translation Candidates

This section gives the definition of the scores of a translation candidate in compositional translation estimation.

First, let y_s be a technical term whose translation is to be estimated. We assume that y_s is de-

[3]Japanese entries are supposed to be segmented into a sequence of words by the morphological analyzer JUMAN (http://www.kc.t.u-tokyo.ac.jp/nl-resource/juman.html).

[4]In our rough estimation, the upper bound of this rate is approximately 80%. An improvement from 69% to 80% could be achieved by extending the bilingual constituents lexicons.

Table 1: Numbers of Entries and Translation Pairs in the Lexicons

lexicon	# of entries		# of translation
	English	Japanese	pairs
Eijiro	1,292,117	1,228,750	1,671,230
P_2	217,861	186,823	235,979
B_P	37,090	34,048	95,568
B_S	20,315	19,345	62,419
B	48,000	42,796	147,848

Eijiro : existing bilingual lexicon
P_2 : entries of Eijiro with two constituents in both languages
B_P : bilingual constituents lexicon (prefix)
B_S : bilingual constituents lexicon (suffix)
B : bilingual constituents lexicon (merged)

composed into their constituents as below:

$$y_s = s_1, s_2, \cdots, s_n \qquad (1)$$

where each s_i is a single word or a sequence of words.[5] For y_s, we denote a generated translation candidate as y_t.

$$y_t = t_1, t_2, \cdots, t_n \qquad (2)$$

where each t_i is a translation of s_i. Then the translation pair $\langle y_s, y_t \rangle$ is represented as follows.

$$\langle y_s, y_t \rangle = \langle s_1, t_1 \rangle, \langle s_2, t_2 \rangle, \cdots, \langle s_n, t_n \rangle \qquad (3)$$

The score of a generated translation candidate is defined as the product of a bilingual lexicon score and a corpus score as follows.

$$Q(y_s, y_t) = Q_{dict}(y_s, y_t) \cdot Q_{coprus}(y_t) \qquad (4)$$

Bilingual lexicon score measures appropriateness of correspondence of y_s and y_t. Corpus score measures appropriateness of the translation candidate y_t based on the target language corpus. If a translation candidate is generated from more than one sequence of translation pairs, the score of the translation candidate is defined as the sum of the score of each sequence.

Bilingual Lexicon Score

In this paper, we compare two types of bilingual lexicon scores. Both scores are defined as the product of scores of translation pairs included in the lexicons presented in the previous section as follows.

[5]Eijiro has both single word entries and compound word entries.

- Frequency-Length

$$Q_{dict}(y_s, y_t) = \prod_{i=1}^{n} q(\langle s_i, t_i \rangle) \qquad (5)$$

The first type of bilingual lexicon scores is referred to as "Frequency-Length." This score is based on the length of translation pairs and the frequencies of translation pairs in the bilingual constituent lexicons (prefix,suffix) B_P, B_S in Table 1. In this paper, we first assume that the translation pairs follow certain preference rules and that they can be ordered as below:

1. Translation pairs $\langle s, t \rangle$ in the existing bilingual lexicon Eijiro, where the term s consists of two or more constituents.
2. Translation pairs in the bilingual constituents lexicons whose frequencies in P_2 are high.
3. Translation pairs $\langle s, t \rangle$ in the existing bilingual lexicon Eijiro, where the term s consists of exactly one constituent.
4. Translation pairs in the bilingual constituents lexicons whose frequencies in P_2 are not high.

As the definition of the confidence score $q(\langle s, t \rangle)$ of a translation pair $\langle s, t \rangle$, we use the following:

$$q(\langle s, t \rangle) = \begin{cases} 10^{(compo(s)-1)} & (\langle s, t \rangle \text{ in Eijiro}) \\ \log_{10} f_p(\langle s, t \rangle) & (\langle s, t \rangle \text{ in } B_P) \\ \log_{10} f_s(\langle s, t \rangle) & (\langle s, t \rangle \text{ in } B_S) \end{cases} \qquad (6)$$

, where $compo(s)$ denotes the word count of s, $f_p(\langle s, t \rangle)$ represents the frequency of $\langle s, t \rangle$ as the first constituent in P_2, and $f_s(\langle s, t \rangle)$ represents the frequency of $\langle s, t \rangle$ as the second constituent in P_2.

- Probability

$$Q_{dict}(y_s, y_t) = \prod_{i=1}^{n} P(s_i | t_i) \qquad (7)$$

The second type of bilingual lexicon scores is referred to as "Probability." This score is calculated as the product of the conditional probabilities $P(s_i|t_i)$. $P(s|t)$ is calculated using bilingual lexicons in Table 1.

$$P(s|t) = \frac{f_{prob}(\langle s, t \rangle)}{\sum_{s_j} f_{prob}(\langle s_j, t \rangle)} \qquad (8)$$

Table 2: 9 Scoring Functions of Translation Candidates and their Components

score ID	bilingual lexicon score		corpus score			corpus	
	freq-length	probability	probability	frequency	occurrence	off-line	on-line (search engine)
A		prune/final	prune/final			o	
B		prune/final		prune/final		o	
C	prune/final		prune/final			o	
D	prune/final				prune	o	
E	prune/final						
F	prune/final			final	prune	o	
G	prune/final			prune/final		o	
H	prune/final			final		o	
I	prune/final			final			o

$f_{prob}(\langle s,t \rangle)$ denotes the frequency of the translation pair $\langle s,t \rangle$ in the bilingual lexicons as follows:

$$f_{prob}(\langle s,t \rangle) = \begin{cases} 10 & (\langle s,t \rangle \text{ in Eijiro}) \\ f_B(\langle s,t \rangle) & (\langle s,t \rangle \text{ in } B) \end{cases} \quad (9)$$

Note that the frequency of a translation pair in Eijiro is regarded as 10[6] and $f_B(\langle s,t \rangle)$ denotes the frequency of the translation pair $\langle s,t \rangle$ in the bilingual constituent lexicon B.

Corpus Score

We evaluate three types of corpus scores as follows.

- Probability: the occurrence probability of y_t estimated by the following bi-gram model

$$Q_{corpus}(y_t) = P(t_1) \cdot \prod_{i=1}^{n} P(t_{i+1}|t_i) \quad (10)$$

- Frequency: the frequency of a translation candidate in a target language corpus

$$Q_{corpus}(y_t) = freq(y_t) \quad (11)$$

- Occurrence: whether a translation candidate occurs in a target language corpus or not

$$Q_{corpus}(y_t) = \begin{cases} 1 & y_t \text{ occurs in a corpus} \\ 0 & y_t \text{ does not occur} \\ & \text{in a corpus} \end{cases} \quad (12)$$

[6] It is necessary to empirically examine whether or not the definition of the frequency of a translation pair in Eijiro is appropriate.

Variation of the total scoring functions

As shown in Table 2, in this paper, we examine the 9 combinations of the bilingual lexicon scores and the corpus scores. In the table, 'prune' indicates that the score is used for ranking and pruning sub-sequences of generated translation candidates in the course of generating translation candidates using a dynamic programming algorithm. 'Final' indicates that the score is used for ranking the final outputs of generating translation candidates. In the column 'corpus', 'off-line' indicates that a domain/topic-specific corpus is collected from the Web in advance and then generated translation candidates are validated against this corpus. 'On-line' indicates that translation candidates are directly validated through the search engine.

Roughly speaking, the scoring function 'A' corresponds to a variant of the model proposed by (Fujii and Ishikawa, 2001). The scoring function 'D' is a variant of the model proposed by (Tonoike et al., 2005) and 'E' corresponds to the bilingual lexicon score of the scoring function 'D'. The scoring function 'I' is intended to evaluate the approach proposed in (Cao and Li, 2002).

3.3.3 Combining Two Scoring Functions based on their Agreement

In this section, we examine the method that combines two scoring functions based on their agreement. The two scoring functions are selected out of the 9 functions introduced in the previous section. In this method, first, confidence of translation candidates of a technical term are measured by the two scoring functions. Then, if the first ranked translation candidates of both scoring functions agree, this method outputs the agreed translation candidate. The purpose of introducing this method is to prefer precision to recall.

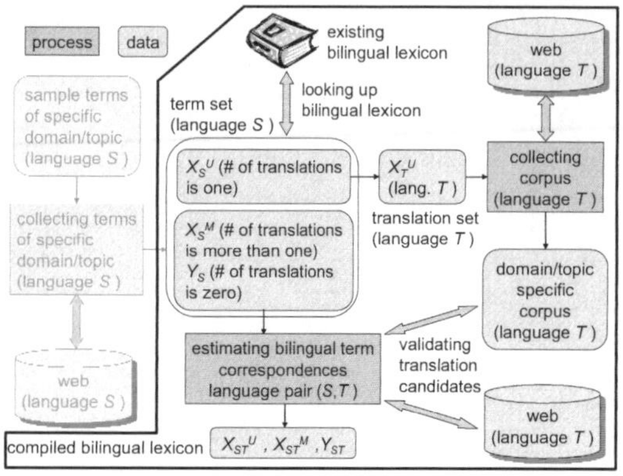

Figure 4: Experimental Evaluation of Translation Estimation for Technical Terms with/without the Domain/Topic-Specific Corpus (taken from Figure 1)

4 Experiments and Evaluation

4.1 Translation Pairs for Evaluation

In our experimental evaluation, within the framework of compiling a bilingual lexicon for technical terms, we evaluate the translation estimation portion that is indicated by the bold line in Figure 4. In this paper, we simply omit the evaluation of the process of collecting technical terms to be listed as the headwords of a bilingual lexicon. In order to evaluate the translation estimation portion, terms are randomly selected from the 10 categories of existing Japanese-English technical term dictionaries listed in Table 3, for each of the subsets X_S^U and Y_S (here, the terms of Y_S that consist of only one word or morpheme are excluded). As described in Section 1, the terms of the set X_T^U (the set of translations for the terms of the subset X_S^U) is used for collecting a domain/topic-specific corpus from the Web. As shown in Table 3, size of the collected corpora is 48MB on the average. Translation estimation evaluation is to be conducted for the subset Y_S. For each of the 10 categories, Table 3 shows the sizes of the subsets X_S^U and Y_S, and the rate of including correct translation within the collected domain/topic-specific corpus for Y_S. In the following, we show the evaluation results with the source language S as English and the target language T as Japanese.

4.2 Evaluation of single scoring functions

This section gives the results of evaluating single scoring functions A $\sim$ I listed in Table 2.

Table 4 shows three types of experimental results. The column 'the whole set Y_S' shows the results against the whole set Y_S. The column 'generatable' shows the results against the translation pairs in Y_S that can be generated through the compositional translation estimation process. 69% of the terms in 'the whole set Y_S' belongs to the set 'generatable'. The column 'gene.-exist' shows the result against the source terms whose correct translations do exist in the corpus and that can be generated through the compositional translation estimation process. 50% of the terms in 'the whole set Y_S' belongs to the set 'gene.-exist'. The column 'top 1' shows the correct rate of the first ranked translation candidate. The column 'top 10' shows the rate of including the correct candidate within top 10.

First, in order to evaluate the effectiveness of the approach of validating translation candidates by using a target language corpus, we compare the scoring functions 'D' and 'E'. The difference between them is whether or not they use a corpus score. The results for the whole set Y_S show that using a corpus score, the precision improves from 33.9% to 43.0%. This result supports the effectiveness of the approach of validating translation candidates using a target language corpus.

As can be seen from these results for the whole set Y_S, the correct rate of the scoring function 'I' that directly uses the web search engine in the calculation of its corpus score is higher than those of other scoring functions that use the collected domain/topic-specific corpus. This is because, for the whole set Y_S, the rate of including correct translation within the collected domain/topic-specific corpus is 72% on the average, which is not very high. On the other hand, the results of the column 'gene.-exist' show that if the correct translation does exist in the corpus, most of the scoring functions other than 'I' can achieve precisions higher than that of the scoring function 'I'. This result supports the effectiveness of the approach of collecting a domain/topic-specific corpus from the Web in advance and then validating generated translation candidates against this corpus.

4.3 Evaluation of combining two scoring functions based on their agreement

The result of evaluating the method that combines two scoring functions based on their agreement is shown in Table 5. This result indicates that combinations of scoring functions with 'off-line'/'on-

Table 3: Number of Translation Pairs for Evaluation (S=English)

dictionaries	categories	$\|Y_S\|$	$\|X_S^U\|$	corpus size	$C(S)$
McGraw-Hill	Electromagnetics	33	36	28MB	85%
	Electrical engineering	45	34	21MB	71%
	Optics	31	42	37MB	65%
Iwanami	Programming language	29	37	34MB	93%
	Programming	29	29	33MB	97%
Dictionary of Computer	(Computer)	100	91	67MB	51%
Dictionary of 250,000 medical terms	Anatomical Terms	100	91	73MB	86%
	Disease	100	91	83MB	77%
	Chemicals and Drugs	100	94	54MB	60%
	Physical Science and Statistics	100	88	56MB	68%
Total		667	633	482MB	72%

McGraw-Hill : Dictionary of Scientific and Technical Terms
Iwanami : Encyclopedic Dictionary of Computer Science
$C(S)$: for Y_S, the rate of including correct translations within the collected domain/topic-specific corpus

Table 4: Result of Evaluating single Scoring Functions

	the whole set Y_S (667 terms$\sim$100%)		generatable (458 terms$\sim$69%)		gene.-exist (333 terms$\sim$50%)	
ID	top 1	top 10	top 1	top 10	top 1	top 10
A	43.8%	52.9%	63.8%	77.1%	82.0%	98.5%
B	42.9%	50.7%	62.4%	73.8%	83.8%	99.4%
C	43.0%	58.0%	62.7%	84.5%	75.1%	94.6%
D	43.0%	47.4%	62.7%	69.0%	**85.9%**	94.6%
E	33.9%	57.3%	49.3%	83.4%	51.1%	84.1%
F	40.2%	47.4%	58.5%	69.0%	80.2%	94.6%
G	39.1%	46.8%	57.0%	68.1%	78.1%	93.4%
H	43.8%	57.3%	63.8%	83.4%	73.6%	84.1%
I	**49.8%**	57.3%	72.5%	83.4%	74.8%	84.1%

Table 5: Result of combining two scoring functions based on their agreement

corpus	combination	precision	recall	$F_{\beta=1}$
off-line/ on-line	A & I	**88.0%**	27.6%	0.420
	D & I	86.0%	29.5%	0.440
	F & I	85.1%	29.1%	0.434
	H & I	58.7%	37.5%	0.457
off-line/ off-line	A & H	**86.0%**	30.4%	0.450
	F & H	80.6%	33.7%	0.476
	D & H	80.4%	32.7%	0.465
	A & D	79.0%	32.1%	0.456
	A & F	74.6%	33.0%	0.457
	D & F	68.2%	35.7%	0.469

line' corpus tend to achieve higher precisions than those with 'off-line'/'off-line' corpus. This result also shows that it is quite possible to achieve high precisions even by combining scoring functions with 'off-line'/'off-line' corpus (the pair 'A' and 'H'). Here, the two scoring functions 'A' and 'H' are the one with frequency-based scoring functions and that with probability-based scoring functions, and hence, have quite different nature in the design of their scoring functions.

5 Related Works

As a related work, (Fujii and Ishikawa, 2001) proposed a technique for compositional estimation of bilingual term correspondences for the purpose of cross-language information retrieval. One of the major differences between the technique of (Fujii and Ishikawa, 2001) and the one proposed in this paper is that in (Fujii and Ishikawa, 2001), instead of a domain/topic-specific corpus, they use a corpus containing the collection of technical papers, each of which is published by one of the 65 Japanese associations for various technical domains. Another significant difference is that in (Fujii and Ishikawa, 2001), they evaluate only the performance of the cross-language information retrieval and not that of translation estimation.

(Cao and Li, 2002) also proposed a method of compositional translation estimation for compounds. In the method of (Cao and Li, 2002), the translation candidates of a term are compositionally generated by concatenating the translation of the constituents of the term and are validated directly through the search engine. In this paper, we evaluate the approach proposed in (Cao and Li, 2002) by introducing a total scoring function that is based on validating translation candidates directly through the search engine.

6 Conclusion

This paper studied issues related to the compilation a bilingual lexicon for technical terms. In the task of estimating bilingual term correspondences of technical terms, it is usually rather difficult to find an existing corpus for the domain of such technical terms. In this paper, we adopt an approach of collecting a corpus for the domain of such technical terms from the Web. As a method of translation estimation for technical terms, we employed a compositional translation estimation technique. This paper focused on quantitatively comparing variations of the components in the scoring functions of compositional translation estimation. Through experimental evaluation, we showed that the domain/topic specific corpus contributes to improving the performance of the compositional translation estimation.

Future work includes complementally integrating the proposed framework of compositional translation estimation using the Web with other translation estimation techniques. One of them is that based on collecting partially bilingual texts through the search engine (Nagata and others, 2001; Huang et al., 2005). Another technique which seems to be useful is that of transliteration of names (Knight and Graehl, 1998; Oh and Choi, 2005).

References

Y. Cao and H. Li. 2002. Base noun phrase translation using Web data and the EM algorithm. In *Proc. 19th COLING*, pages 127–133.

A. Fujii and T. Ishikawa. 2001. Japanese/english cross-language information retrieval: Exploration of query translation and transliteration. *Computers and the Humanities*, 35(4):389–420.

P. Fung and L. Y. Yee. 1998. An IR approach for translating new words from nonparallel, comparable texts. In *Proc. 17th COLING and 36th ACL*, pages 414–420.

F. Huang, Y. Zhang, and S. Vogel. 2005. Mining key phrase translations from web corpora. In *Proc. HLT/EMNLP*, pages 483–490.

K. Knight and J. Graehl. 1998. Machine transliteration. *Computational Linguistics*, 24(4):599–612.

Y. Matsumoto and T. Utsuro. 2000. Lexical knowledge acquisition. In R. Dale, H. Moisl, and H. Somers, editors, Handbook of Natural Language Processing, chapter 24, pages 563–610. Marcel Dekker Inc.

M. Nagata et al. 2001. Using the Web as a bilingual dictionary. In *Proc. ACL-2001 Workshop on Data-driven Methods in Machine Translation*, pages 95–102.

J. Oh and K. Choi. 2005. Automatic extraction of english-korean translations for constituents of technical terms. In *Proc. 2nd IJCNLP*, pages 450–461.

R. Rapp. 1999. Automatic identification of word translations from unrelated English and German corpora. In *Proc. 37th ACL*, pages 519–526.

S. Sato and Y. Sasaki. 2003. Automatic collection of related terms from the web. In *Proc. 41st ACL*, pages 121–124.

T. Tanaka and T. Baldwin. 2003. Translation selection for japanese-english noun-noun compounds. In *Proc. Machine Translation Summit IX*, pages 378–85.

M. Tonoike, M. Kida, T. Takagi, Y. Sasaki, T. Utsuro, and S. Sato. 2005. Effect of domain-specific corpus in compositional translation estimation for technical terms. In *Proc. 2nd IJCNLP, Companion Volume*, pages 116–121.

CUCWeb: a Catalan corpus built from the Web

G. Boleda[1] **S. Bott**[1] **R. Meza**[2] **C. Castillo**[2] **T. Badia**[1] **V. López**[2]
[1]Grup de Lingüística Computacional
[2]Cátedra Telefónica de Producción Multimedia
Fundació Barcelona Media
Universitat Pompeu Fabra
Barcelona, Spain
{gemma.boleda,stefan.bott,rodrigo.meza}@upf.edu
{carlos.castillo,toni.badia,vicente.lopez}@upf.edu

Abstract

This paper presents CUCWeb, a 166 million word corpus for Catalan built by crawling the Web. The corpus has been annotated with NLP tools and made available to language users through a flexible web interface. The developed architecture is quite general, so that it can be used to create corpora for other languages.

1 Introduction

CUCWeb is the outcome of the common interest of two groups, a Computational Linguistics group and a Computer Science group interested on Web studies. It fits into a larger project, The Spanish Web Project, aimed at empirically studying the properties of the Spanish Web (Baeza-Yates et al., 2005). The project set up an architecture to retrieve a portion of the Web roughly corresponding to the Web in Spain, in order to study its formal properties (analysing its link distribution as a graph) and its characteristics in terms of pages, sites, and domains (size, kind of software used, language, among other aspects).

One of the by-products of the project is a 166 million word corpus for Catalan.[1] The biggest annotated Catalan corpus before CUCWeb is the CTILC corpus (Rafel, 1994), consisting of about 50 million words.

In recent years, the Web has been increasingly used as a source of linguistic data (Kilgarriff and Grefenstette, 2003). The most straightforward approach to using the Web as corpus is to gather data online (Grefenstette, 1998), or estimate counts (Keller and Lapata, 2003) using available search engines. This approach has a number of drawbacks, e.g. the data one looks for has to be known beforehand, and the queries have to consist of lexical material. In other words, it is not possible to perform structural searches or proper language modeling.

Current technology makes it feasible and relatively cheap to crawl and store terabytes of data. In addition, crawling the data and processing it off-line provides more potential for its exploitation, as well as more control over the data selection and pruning processes. However, this approach is more challenging from a technological viewpoint. [2] For a comprehensive discussion of the pros and cons of the different approaches to using Web data for linguistic purposes, see e.g. Thelwall (2005) and Lüdeling et al. (To appear). We chose the second approach because of the advantages discussed in this section, and because it allowed us to make the data available for a large number of non-specialised users, through a web interface to the corpus. We built a general-purpose corpus by crawling the Spanish Web, processing and filtering them with language-intensive tools, filtering duplicates and ranking them according to popularity.

The paper has the following structure: Section 2 details the process that lead to the constitution of the corpus, Section 3 explores some of the exploitation possibilities that are foreseen for CUCWeb, and Section 4 discusses the current architecture. Finally, Section 5 contains some conclusions and future work.

[1]Catalan is a relatively minor language. There are currently about 10.8 million Catalan speakers, similar to Serbian (12), Greek (10.2), or Swedish (9.3). See http://www.upc.es/slt/alatac/cat/dades/catala-04.html

[2]The WaCky project (http://wacky.sslmit.unibo.it/) aims at overcoming this challenge, by developing "a set of tools (and interfaces to existing tools) that will allow a linguist to crawl a section of the web, process the data, index them and search them".

2 Corpus Constitution

2.1 Data collection

Our goal was to crawl the portion of the Web related to Spain. Initially, we crawled the set of pages with the suffix `.es`. However, this domain is not very popular, because it is more expensive than other domains (e.g. the cost of a `.com` domain is about 15% of that of an `.es` domain), and because its use is restricted to company names or registered trade marks.[3] In a second phase a different heuristic was used, and we considered that a Web site was in Spain if either its IP address was assigned to a network located in Spanish land, or if the Web site's suffix was `.es`. We found that only 16% of the domains with pages in Spain were under `.es`.

The final collection of the data was carried out in September and October 2004, using a commercial piece of software by Akwan (da Silva et al., 1999). [4] The actual collection was started by the crawler using as a seed the list of URLs in a Spanish search engine –which was a commercial search engine back in 2000– under the name of Buscopio. That list covered the major part of the existing Web in Spain at that time. [5]. New URLs were extracted from the downloaded pages, and the process continued recursively while the pages *were in Spain* –see above. The crawler downloaded all pages, except those that had an identical URL (`http://www.web.es/main/` and `http://www.web.es/main/index.html` were considered different URLs). We retrieved over 16 million Web pages (corresponding to over 300,000 web sites and 118,000 domains), and processed them to extract links and text. The uncompressed text of the pages amounts to 46 GB, and the metadata generated during the crawl to 3 GB.

In an initial collection process, a number of difficulties in the characterisation of the Web of Spain were identified, which lead to redundancy in the contents of the collection:

Parameters to a program inside URL addresses. This makes it impossible to adequately separate static and dynamic pages, and may lead to repeatedly crawl pages with the same content.

Mirrors (geographically distributed copies of the same contents to ensure network efficiency). Normally, these replicas are entire collections with a large volume, so that there are many sites with the same contents, and these are usually large sites. The replicated information is estimated between 20% and 40% of the total Web contents ((Baeza-Yates et al., 2005)).

Spam on the Web (actions oriented to deceive search engines and to give to some pages a higher ranking than they deserve in search results). Recognizing spam pages is an active research area, and it is estimated that over 8% of what is indexed by search engines is spam (Fetterly et al., 2004). One of the strategies that induces redundancy is to automatically generate pages to improve the score they obtain in link-based rankings algorithms.

DNS wildcarding (domain name spamming). Some link analysis ranking functions assign less importance to links between pages in the same Web site. Unfortunately, this has motivated spammers to use several different Web sites for the same contents, usually through configuring DNS servers to assign hundreds or thousands of site names to the same IP address. Spain's Web seems to be quite populated with domain name spammers: 24 out of the 30 domains with the highest number of Web sites are configured with DNS wildcarding (Baeza-Yates et al., 2005).

Most of the spam pages were under the `.com` top-level domain. We manually checked the domains with the largest number of sites and pages to ban a list of them, mostly sites containing pornography or collections of links without information content. This is not a perfect solution against spam, but generates significant savings in terms of bandwidth and storage, and allows us to spend more resources in content-rich Web sites. We also restricted the crawler to download a maximum of 400 pages per site, except for the Web sites within `.es`, that had no pre-established limit.

[3]In the case of Catalan, additionally, there is a political and cultural opposition to the `.es` domain.

[4]We used a PC with two Intel-4 processors running at 3 GHz and with 1.6 GB of RAM under Red-Hat Linux. For the information storage we used a RAID of disks with 1.8 TB of total capacity, although the space used by the collection is about 50 GB.

[5]http://www.buscopio.net

	Documents	(%)	Words	(%)
Language classifier	491,850	100	375,469,518	100
Dictionary filter	277,577	56.5	222,363,299	59
Duplicate detector	204,238	41.5	166,040,067	44

Table 1: Size of the Catalan corpus

2.2 Data processing

The processing of the data to obtain the Catalan corpus consisted of the following steps: language classification, linguistic filtering and processing, duplicate filtering and corpus indexing. This section details each of these aspects.

We built a language classifier with the Naive Bayes classifier of the Bow system (Mccallum, 1996). The system was trained with corpora corresponding to the 4 official languages in Spain (Spanish, Catalan, Galician and Basque), as well as to the other 6 most frequent languages in the Web (Anonymous, 2000): English, German, French, Italian, Portuguese, and Dutch.

38% of the collection could not be reliably classified, mostly because of the presence of pages without enough text, for instance, pages containing only images or only lists of proper nouns. Within the classified pages, Catalan was the third most used language (8% of the collection). As expected, most of the collection was in Spanish (52%), but English had a large part (31%). The contents in Galician and Basque only comprise about 2% of the pages.

We wanted to use the Catalan portion as a corpus for NLP and linguistic studies. We were not interested in full coverage of Web data, but in quality. Therefore, we filtered it using a computational dictionary and some heuristics in order to exclude documents with little linguistic relevance (e.g. address lists) or with a lot of noise (programming code, multilingual documents). In addition, we performed a simple duplicate filter: web pages with a very similar content (determined by a hash of the processed text) were considered duplicates.

The sizes of the corpus (in documents and words[6]) after each of the processes are depicted in Table 1. Note that the two filtering processes discard almost 60% of the original documents. The final corpus consists of 166 million words from 204 thousand documents.

Its distribution in terms of top-level domains is shown in Table 2, and the 10 biggest sites in Table 3. Note that the `.es` domain covers almost half of the pages and `com` a quarter, but `.org` and `.net` also have a quite large share of the pages. As for the biggest sites, they give an idea of the content of CUCWeb: they mainly correspond to university and institutional sites. A similar distribution can be observed for the 50 biggest sites, which will determine the kind of language found in CUCWeb.

	Documents	(%)
es	89,541	44.6
com	49,146	24.5
org	35,528	17.7
net	18,819	9.4
info	5,005	2.5
edu	688	0.3
others	2,042	1.4

Table 2: Domain distribution in CUCWeb

The corpus was further processed with CatCG (Àlex Alsina et al., 2002), a POS-tagger and shallow parser for Catalan built with the Connexor Constraint Grammar formalism and tools.[7] CatCG provides part of speech, morphological features (gender, number, tense, etc.) and syntactic information. The syntactic information is a functional tag (e.g. subject, object, main verb) annotated at word level.

Since we wanted the corpus not only to be an in-house resource for NLP purposes, but also to be accessible to a large number of users. To that end, we indexed it using the IMS Corpus Workbench tools[8] and we built a web interface to it (see Section 3.1). The CWB includes facilities for indexing and searching corpora, as well as a special module for web interfaces. However, the size of the corpus is above the advisable limit for these tools. [9] Therefore, we divided it into 4 subcorpora

[6]Word counts do not include punctuation marks.

[7]http://www.connexor.com/

[8]http://www.ims.uni-stuttgart.de/projekte/CorpusWorkbench/

[9]According to Stefan Evert –personal communication–, if a corpus has to be split into several parts, a good rule of thumb is to split it in 100M word parts. In his words "depending on various factors such as language, complexity of annotations

Site	Description	Documents
upc.es	University	1574
gencat.es	Institution	1372
publicacions.bcn.es	Institution	1282
uab.es	University	1190
revista.consumer.es	Company	1132
upf.es	University	1076
nil.fut.es	Distribution lists	1045
conc.es	Insitution	1033
uib.es	University	977
ajtarragona.es	Institution	956

Table 3: 10 biggest sites in CUCWeb

and indexed each of them separately. The search engine for the corpus is the CQP (Corpus Query Processor, one of the modules of the CWB).

Since CQP provides sequential access to documents we ordered the corpus documents by PageRank so that they are retrieved according to their popularity on the Internet.

3 Corpus Exploitation

CUCWeb is being exploited in two ways: on the one hand, data can be accessed through a web interface (Section 3.1). On the other hand, the annotated data can be exploited by theoretical or computational linguists, lexicographers, translators, etc. (Section 3.2).

3.1 Corpus interface

Despite the wide use of corpora in NLP, few interfaces have been built, and still fewer are flexible enough to be of interest to linguistic researchers. As for Web data, some initiatives exist (WebCorp [10], the Linguist's Search Engine [11], KWiCFinder [12]), but they are meta-interfaces to search engines. For Catalan, there is a web interface for the CTILC corpus[13], but it only allows for one word searches, of which a maximum of 50 hits are viewed. It is not possible either to download search results.

From the beginning of the project our aim was to create a corpus which could be useful for both the NLP community and for a more general audience with an interest in the Catalan language. This includes linguists, lexicographers and language teachers.

We expected the latter kind of user not to be familiar with corpus searching strategies and corpus interfaces, at least not to a large extent. Therefore, we aimed at creating a user-friendly web interface which should be useful for both non-trained and experienced users.[14] Further on, we wanted the interface to support not only example searches but also statistical information, such as co-occurrence frequency, of use in lexicographical work and potentially also in language teaching or learning.

There are two web interfaces to the corpus: an example search interface and a statistics interface. Furthermore, since the flexibility and expressiveness of the searches potentially conflicts with user-friendliness, we decided to divide the example search interface into two modalities: a simple search mode and an expert search mode.

The simple mode allows for searches of words, lemmata or word strings. The search can be restricted to specific parts of speech or syntactic functions. For instance, a user can search for an ambiguous word like Catalan "la" (masculine noun, or feminine determiner or personal pronoun) and restrict the search to pronouns. Or look for word "traduccions" ('translations') functioning as subject. The advantage of the simple mode is that an untrained person can use the corpus almost without the need to read instructions. If new users find it useful to use CUCWeb, we expect that the motivation to learn how to create advanced corpus queries will arise.

The expert mode is somewhat more complex but very flexible. A string of up to 5 word units can be searched, where each unit may be a word

and how much RAM you have, a larger or smaller size may give better overall performance.".

[10]http://www.webcorp.org.uk/

[11]http://lse.umiacs.umd.edu

[12]http://miniappolis.com/KWiCFinder

[13]http://pdl.iec.es

[14]http://www.catedratelefonica.upf.es/cucweb

form, lemma, part of speech, syntactic function or combination of any of those. If a part of speech is specified, further morphological information is displayed, which can also be queried.

Each word unit can be marked as optional or repeated, which corresponds to the Boolean operators of repetition and optionality. Within each word unit each information field may be negated, allowing for exclusions in searches, e.g. requiring a unit not to be a noun or not corresponding to a certain lemma. This use of operators gives the expert mode an expressiveness close to regular grammars, and exploits almost all querying functionalities of CQP –the search engine.

In both modes, the user can retrieve up to 1000 examples, which can be viewed online or downloaded as a text file, and with different context sizes. In addition, a link to a cache copy of the document and to its original location is provided.

As for the statistics interface, it searches for frequency information regarding the query of the user. The frequency can be related to any of the 4 annotation levels (word, lemma, POS, function). For example, it is possible to search for a given verb lemma and get the frequencies of each verb form, or to look for adjectives modifying the word *dona* ('woman') and obtain the list of lemmata with their associated frequency. The results are offered as a table with absolute and relative frequency, and they can be viewed online or retrieved as a CSV file. In addition, each of the results has an associated link to the actual examples in the corpus.

The interface is technically quite complex, and the corpus quite large. There are still aspects to be solved both in the implementation and the documentation of the interface. Even restricting the searches to 1000 hits, efficiency remains often a problem in the example search mode, and more so in the statistics interface. Two partial solutions have been adopted so far: first, to divide the corpus into 4 subcorpora, as explained in Section 2.2, so that parallel searches can be performed and thus the search engine is not as often overloaded. Second, to limit the amount of memory and time for a given query. In the statistics interface, a status bar shows the progress of the query in percentage and the time left.

The interface does not offer the full range of CWB/CQP functionalities, mainly because it was not demanded by our "known" users (most of them linguists and translators from the Department of Translation and Philology at Universitat Pompeu Fabra). However it is planned to increasingly add new features and functionalities. Up to now we did not detect any incompatibility between splitting the corpora and the implementation of CWB/CQP deployment or querying functionalities.

3.2 Whole dataset

The annotated corpus can be used as a source of data for NLP purposes. A previous version of the CUCWeb corpus –obtained with the methodology described in this paper, but crawling only the `.es` domain, consisting of 180 million words– has already been exploited in a lexical acquisition task, aimed at classifying Catalan verbs into syntactic classes (Mayol et al., 2006).

Cluster analysis was applied to a 200 verb set, modeled in terms of 10 linguistically defined features. The data for the clustering were first extracted from a fragment of CTILC (14 million word). Using the manual tagging of the corpus, an average 0.84 f-score was obtained. Using CatCG, the performance decreased only 2 points (0.82 f-score).

In a subsequent experiment, the data were extracted from the CUCWeb corpus. Given that it is 12 times larger than the traditional corpus, the question was whether "more data is better data" (Church and Mercer, 1993, 18-19). Banko and Brill (2001) present a case study on confusion set disambiguation that supports this slogan. Surprisingly enough, results using CUCWeb were significantly worse than those using the traditional corpus, even with automatic linguistic processing: CUCWeb lead to an average 0.71 f-score, so an 11 point difference resulted. These results somewhat question the quality of the CUCWeb corpus, particularly so as the authors attribute the difference to noise in the CUCWeb and difficulties in linguistic processing (see Section 4). However, 0.71 is still well beyond the 0.33 f-score baseline, so that our analysis is that CUCWeb can be successfully used in lexical acquisition tasks. Improvement in both filtering and linguistic processing is still a must, though.

4 Discussion of the architecture

The initial motivation for the CUCWeb project was to obtain a large annotated corpus for Catalan. However, we set up an architecture that enables

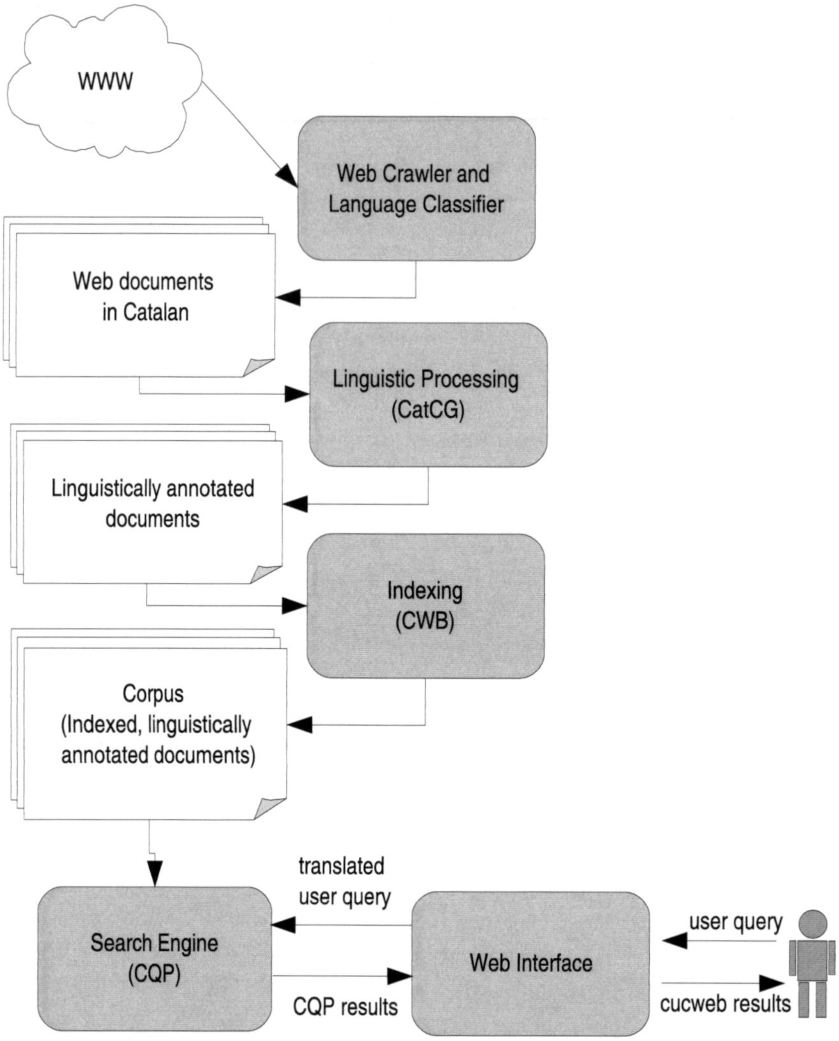

Figure 1: Architecture for building Web corpora

the construction of web corpora in general, provided the language-dependent modules are available. Figure 1 shows the current architecture for CUCWeb.

The language-dependent modules are the language classifier (our classifier now covers 10 languages, as explained in Section 2.2) and the linguistic processing tools. In addition, the web interface has to be adapted for each new tagset, piece of information and linguistic level. For instance, the interface currently does not support searches for chunks or phrases.

Most of the problems we have encountered in processing Web documents are not new (Baroni and Ueyama, To appear), but they are much more frequent in that kind of documents than in standard running text.[15] We now review the main problems we came across:

Textual layout In general, they are problems that arise due to the layout of Web documents, which is very different to that of standard text. Pre-processing tools have to be adapted to deal with these elements. These include headers or footers (*Last modified...*), copyright statements or frame elements, the so-called *boilerplates*. Currently, due to the fact that we process the text extracted by the crawler, no boilerplate detection is performed, which increases the amount of noise in the corpus. Moreover, the pre-processing module does not even handle e-mail addresses or phone numbers (they are not frequently found in the kind of

[15]By "standard text", we mean edited pieces of text, such as newspapers, novels, encyclopedia, or technical manuals.

text it was designed to process); as a result, for example, one of the most frequent determiners in the corpus is *93*, the phone prefix for Barcelona. Another problem for the pre-processing module, again due to the fact that we process the text extracted from the HTML markup, is that most of the structural information is lost and many segmentation errors occur, errors that carry over to subsequent modules.

Spelling mistakes Most of the texts published on the Web are only edited once, by their author, and are neither reviewed nor corrected, as is usually the case in traditional textual collections (Baeza-Yates et al., 2005). It could be argued that this makes the language on the Web closer to the "actual language", or at least representative of other varieties in contrast to traditional corpora. However, this feature makes Web documents difficult to process for NLP purposes, due to the large quantity of spelling mistakes of all kinds. The HTML support itself causes some of the difficulties that are not exactly spelling mistakes: A particularly frequent kind of problem we have found is that the first letter of a word gets segmented from the rest of the word, mainly due to formatting effects. Automatic spelling correction is a more necessary module in the case of Web data.

Multilinguality Multilinguality is also not a new issue (there are indeed multilingual books or journals), but is one that becomes much more evident when handling Web documents. Our current approach, given that we are not interested in full coverage, but in quality, is to discard multilingual documents (through the language classifier and the linguistic filter). This causes two problems. On the one hand, potentially useful texts are lost, if they are inserted in multilingual documents (note that the linguistic filter reduces the initial collection to almost a half; see Table 1). On the other hand, many multilingual documents remain in the corpus, because the amount of text in another language does not reach the specified threshold. Due to the sociological context of Catalan, Spanish-Catalan documents are particularly frequent, and this can cause trouble in e.g. lexical acquisition tasks, because both are Romance languages and some word forms coincide. Currently, both the language classifier and the dictionary filter are document-based, not sentence-based. A better approach would be to do sentence-based language classification. However, this would increase the complexity of corpus construction and management: If we want to maintain the notion of document, pieces in other languages have to be marked but not removed. Ideally, they should also be tagged and subsequently made searchable.

Duplicates Finally, a problem which is indeed particular to the Web is redundancy. Despite all efforts in avoiding duplicates during the crawling and in detecting them in the collection (see Section 2), there is still quite a lot of duplicates or near-duplicates in the corpus. This is a problem both for NLP purposes and for corpus querying. More sophisticated algorithms, as in Broder (2000), are needed to improve duplicate detection.

5 Conclusions and future work

We have presented CUCWeb, a project aimed at obtaining a large Catalan corpus from the Web and making it available for all language users. As an existing resource, it is possible to enhance it and modify it, with e.g. better filters, better duplicate detectors, or better NLP tools. Having an actual corpus stored and annotated also makes it possible to explore it, be it through the web interface or as a dataset.

The first CUCWeb version (from data gathering to linguistic processing and web interface implementation) was developed in only 6 months, with partial dedication of a a team of 6 people. Since then, many improvements have taken place, and many more remain as a challenge, but it confirms that creating a 166 million word annotated corpus, given the current technological state of the art, is a relatively easy and cheap issue.

Resources such as CUCWeb facilitate the technological development of non-major languages and quantitative linguistic research, particularly so if flexible web interfaces are implemented. In addition, they make it possible for NLP and Web studies to converge, opening new fields of research (e.g. sociolinguistic studies of the Web).

We have argued that the developed architecture allows for the creation of Web corpora in general. In fact, in the near future we plan to build a Spanish Web corpus and integrate it into the same web interface, using the data already gathered. The Spanish corpus, however, will be much larger than the Catalan one (a conservative estimate is 600 million words), so that new challenges in processing and searching it will arise.

We have also reviewed some of the challenges that Web data pose to existing NLP tools, and argued that most are not new (textual layout, misspellings, multilinguality), but more frequent on the Web. To address some of them, we plan to develop a more sophisticated pre-processing module and a sentence-based language classifier and filter.

A more general challenge of Web corpora is the control over its contents. Unlike traditional corpora, where the origin of each text is clear and deliberate, in CUCWeb the strategy is to gather as much text as possible, provided it meets some quality heuristics. The notion of balance is not present anymore, although this needs not be a drawback (Web corpora are at least representative of the language on the Web). However, what is arguably a drawback is the black box effect of the corpus, because the impact of text genre, topic, and so on cannot be taken into account. It would require a text classification procedure to know what the collected corpus contains, and this is again a meeting point for Web studies and NLP.

Acknowledgements

María Eugenia Fuenmayor and Paulo Golgher managed the Web crawler during the downloading process. The language classifier was developed by Bárbara Poblete. The corpora used to train the language detection module were kindly provided by Universität Gesamthochschule, Paderborn (German), by the Institut d'Estudis Catalans, Barcelona (Catalan), by the TALP group, Universitat Politècnica de Catalunya (Spanish), by the IXA Group, Euskal Herriko Unibertsitatea (Basque), by the Centre de Traitement Automatique du Langage de l'UCL, Leuven (French, Dutch and Portuguese), by the Seminario de Lingüística Informática, Universidade de Vigo (Galician) and by the Istituto di Linguistica Computazionale, Pisa (Italian). We thank Martí Quixal for his revision of a previous version of this paper and three anonymous reviewers for useful criticism.

This project has been partially funded by Cátedra Telefónica de Producción Multimedia.

References

Àlex Alsina, Toni Badia, Gemma Boleda, Stefan Bott, Àngel Gil, Martí Quixal, and Oriol Valentín. 2002. CATCG: a general purpose parsing tool applied. In *Proceedings of Third International Conference on Language Resources and Evaluation*, Las Palmas, Spain.

Anonymous. 2000. 1.6 billion served: the Web according to Google. *Wired*, 8(12):18–19.

Ricardo Baeza-Yates, Carlos Castillo, and Vicente López. 2005. Characteristics of the Web of Spain. *Cybermetrics*, 9(1).

Michele Banko and Eric Brill. 2001. Scaling to very very large corpora for natural language disambiguation. In *Association for Computational Linguistics*, pages 26–33.

Marco Baroni and Motoko Ueyama. To appear. Building general- and special-purpose corpora by web crawling. In *Proceedings of the NIJL International Workshop on Language Corpora*.

Andrei Z. Broder. 2000. Identifying and filtering near-duplicate documents. In *Combinatorial Pattern Matching, 11th Annual Symposium*, pages 1–10, Montreal, Canada.

Kenneth W. Church and Robert L. Mercer. 1993. Introduction to the special issue on computational linguistics using large corpora. *Computational Linguistics*, 19(1):1–24.

Altigran da Silva, Eveline Veloso, Paulo Golgher, Alberto Laender, and Nivio Ziviani. 1999. Cobweb - a crawler for the brazilian web. In *String Processing and Information Retrieval (SPIRE)*, pages 184–191, Cancun, Mexico. IEEE CS Press.

Dennis Fetterly, Mark Manasse, and Marc Najork. 2004. Spam, damn spam, and statistics: Using statistical analysis to locate spam web pages. In *Seventh workshop on the Web and databases (WebDB)*, Paris, France.

Gregory Grefenstette. 1998. The World Wide Web as a resource for example-based machine translation tasks. In *ASLIB Conference on Translating and the Computer*, volume 21, London, England.

Frank Keller and Mirella Lapata. 2003. Using the web to obtain frequencies for unseen bigrams. *Computational Linguistics*, 29:459–484.

Adam Kilgarriff and Gregory Grefenstette. 2003. Introduction to the special issue on the Web as corpus. *Computational Linguistics*, 29(3):333–347.

Anke Lüdeling, Stefan Evert, and Marco Baroni. To appear. Using web data for linguistic purposes. In Marianne Hundt, Caroline Biewer, and Nadja Nesselhauf, editors, *Corpus Linguistics and the Web*. Rodopi, Amsterdam.

Laia Mayol, Gemma Boleda, and Toni Badia. 2006. Automatic acquisition of syntactic verb classes with basic resources. Submitted.

Andrew K. Mccallum. 1996. Bow: A toolkit for statistical language modeling, text retrieval, classification and clustering. <http://www.cs.cmu.edu/~mccallum/bow/>.

Joaquim Rafel. 1994. Un corpus general de referència de la llengua catalana. *Caplletra*, 17:219–250.

Mike Thelwall. 2005. Creating and using web corpora. *International Journal of Corpus Linguistics*, 10(4):517–541.

Annotated web as corpus

Paul Rayson
Computing Department,
Lancaster University, UK
p.rayson@lancs.ac.uk

James Walkerdine
Computing Department,
Lancaster University, UK
j.walkerdine@lancs.ac.uk

William H. Fletcher
United States Naval
Academy, USA
fletcher@usna.edu

Adam Kilgarriff
Lexical Computing Ltd., UK
adam@lexmasterclass.com

Abstract

This paper presents a proposal to facilitate the use of the *annotated web as corpus* by alleviating the annotation bottleneck for corpus data drawn from the web. We describe a framework for large-scale distributed corpus annotation using peer-to-peer (P2P) technology to meet this need. We also propose to annotate a large reference corpus in order to evaluate this framework. This will allow us to investigate the affordances offered by distributed techniques to ensure replicability of linguistic research based on web-derived corpora.

1 Introduction

Linguistic annotation of corpora contributes crucially to the study of language at several levels: morphology, syntax, semantics, and discourse. Its significance is reflected both in the growing interest in annotation software for word sense tagging (Edmonds and Kilgarriff, 2002) and in the long-standing use of part-of-speech taggers, parsers and morphological analysers for data from English and many other languages.

Linguists, lexicographers, social scientists and other researchers are using ever larger amounts of corpus data in their studies. In corpus linguistics the progression has been from the 1 million-word Brown and LOB corpora of the 1960s, to the 100 million-word British National Corpus of the 1990s. In lexicography this progression is paralleled, for example, by Collins Dictionaries' initial 10 million word corpus growing to their current corpus of around 600 million words. In addition, the requirement for *mega-* and even *giga-corpora*[1] extends to other applications, such as lexical frequency studies, neologism research, and statistical natural language processing where models of sparse data are built. The motivation for increasingly large data sets remains the same. Due to the Zipfian nature of word frequencies, around half the word types in a corpus occur only once, so tremendous increases in corpus size are required both to ensure inclusion of essential word and phrase types and to increase the chances of multiple occurrences of a given type.

In corpus linguistics building such mega-corpora is beyond the scope of individual researchers, and they are not easily accessible (Kennedy, 1998: 56) unless the web is used as a corpus (Kilgarriff and Grefenstette, 2003). Increasingly, corpus researchers are tapping the Web to overcome the sparse data problem (Keller et al., 2002). This topic generated intense interest at workshops held at the University of Heidelberg (October 2004), University of Bologna (January 2005), University of Birmingham (July 2005) and now in Trento in April 2006. In addition, the advantages of using linguistically annotated data over raw data are well documented (Mair, 2005; Granger and Rayson, 1998). As the size of a corpus increases, a near linear increase in computing power is required to annotate the text. Although processing power is steadily growing, it has already become impractical for a single computer to annotate a mega-corpus.

Creating a large-scale annotated corpus from the web requires a way to overcome the limitations on processing power. We propose distributed techniques to alleviate the limitations on the

[1] See, for example, those distributed by the Linguistic Data Consortium: http://www.ldc.upenn.edu/

volume of data that can be tagged by a single processor. The task of annotating the data will be shared by computers at collaborating institutions around the world, taking advantage of processing power and bandwidth that would otherwise go unused. Such large-scale parallel processing removes the workload bottleneck imposed by a server based structure. This allows for tagging a greater amount of textual data in a given amount of time while permitting other users to use the system simultaneously. Vast amounts of data can be analysed with distributed techniques. The feasibility of this approach has been demonstrated by the SETI@home project[2].

The framework we propose can incorporate other annotation or analysis systems, for example, lemmatisation, frequency profiling, or shallow parsing. To realise and evaluate the framework, it will be developed for a peer-to-peer (P2P) network and deployed along with an existing lexicographic toolset, the Sketch Engine. A P2P approach allows for a low cost implementation that draws upon available resources (existing user PCs). As a case study for evaluation, we plan to collect a large reference corpus from the web to be hosted on servers from Lexical Computing Ltd. We can evaluate annotation speed gains of our approach comparatively against the single server version by utilising processing power in computer labs at Lancaster University and the United States Naval Academy (USNA) and we will call for volunteers from the corpus community to be involved in the evaluation as well.

A key aspect of our case study research will be to investigate extending corpus collection to new document types. Most web-derived corpora have exploited raw text or HTML pages, so efforts have focussed on boilerplate removal and clean-up of these formats with tools like Hyppia-BTE, Tidy and Parcels[3] (Baroni and Sharoff, 2005). Other document formats such as Adobe PDF and MS-Word have been neglected due to the extra conversion and clean-up problems they entail. By excluding PDF documents, web-derived corpora are less representative of certain genres such as academic writing.

2 Related Work

The vast majority of previous work on corpus annotation has utilised either manual coding or automated software tagging systems, or else a semi-automatic combination of the two approaches e.g. automated tagging followed by manual correction. In most cases a stand-alone system or client-server approach has been taken by annotation software using batch processing techniques to tag corpora. Only a handful of web-based or email services (CLAWS[4], Amalgam[5], Connexor[6]) are available, for example, in the application of part-of-speech tags to corpora. Existing tagging systems are 'small scale' and typically impose some limitation to prevent overload (e.g. restricted access or document size). Larger systems to support multiple document tagging processes would require resources that cannot be realistically provided by existing single-server systems. This corpus annotation bottleneck becomes even more problematic for voluminous data sets drawn from the web. The use of the web as a corpus for teaching and research on language has been proposed a number of times (Kilgarriff, 2001; Robb, 2003; Rundell, 2000; Fletcher, 2001, 2004b) and received a special issue of the journal *Computational Linguistics* (Kilgarriff and Grefenstette, 2003). Studies have used several different methods to mine web data. Turney (2001) extracts word co-occurrence probabilities from unlabelled text collected from a web crawler. Baroni and Bernardini (2004) built a corpus by iteratively searching Google for a small set of seed terms. Prototypes of Internet search engines for linguists, corpus linguists and lexicographers have been proposed: WebCorp (Kehoe and Renouf, 2002), KWiCFinder (Fletcher, 2004a) and the Linguist's Search Engine (Kilgarriff, 2003; Resnik and Elkiss, 2003).

A key concern in corpus linguistics and related disciplines is verifiability and replicability of the results of studies. Word frequency counts in internet search engines are inconsistent and unreliable (Veronis, 2005). Tools based on static corpora do not suffer from this problem, e.g. BNCweb[7], developed at the University of Zurich, and View[8] (Variation in English Words and Phrases, developed at Brigham Young University)

[2] http://setiathome.ssl.berkeley.edu/

[3] http://www.smi.ucd.ie/hyppia/, http://parcels.sourceforge.net and http://tidy.sourceforge.net.

[4] http://www.comp.lancs.ac.uk/ucrel/claws/trial.html

[5] http://www.comp.leeds.ac.uk/amalgam/amalgam/amalghome.htm

[6] http://www.connexor.com

[7] http://homepage.mac.com/bncweb/home.html

[8] http://view.byu.edu/

are both based on the British National Corpus. Both BNCweb and View enable access to annotated corpora and facilitate searching on part-of-speech tags. In addition, PIE[9] (Phrases in English), developed at USNA, which performs searches on n-grams (based on words, parts-of-speech and characters), is currently restricted to the British National Corpus as well, although other static corpora are being added to its database. In contrast, little progress has been made toward annotating sizable sample corpora from the web.

"Real-time" linguistic analysis of web data at the syntactic level has been piloted by the Linguist's Search Engine (LSE). Using this tool, linguists can either perform syntactic searches via parse trees on a pre-analysed web collection of around three million sentences from the Internet Archive (www.archive.org) or build their own collections from AltaVista search engine results. The second method pushes the new collection onto a queue for the LSE annotator to analyse. A new collection does not become available for analysis until the LSE completes the annotation process, which may entail significant delay with multiple users of the LSE server. The Gsearch system (Corley et al., 2001) also selects sentences by syntactic criteria from large on-line text collections. Gsearch annotates corpora with a fast chart parser to obviate the need for corpora with pre-existing syntactic mark-up. In contrast, the Sketch Engine system to assist lexicographers to construct dictionary entries requires large pre-annotated corpora. A word sketch is an automatic one-page corpus-derived summary of a word's grammatical and collocational behaviour. Word Sketches were first used to prepare the Macmillan English Dictionary for Advanced Learners (2002, edited by Michael Rundell). They have also served as the starting point for high-accuracy Word Sense Disambiguation. More recently, the Sketch Engine was used to develop the new edition of the Oxford Thesaurus of English (2004, edited by Maurice Waite).

Parallelising or distributing processing has been suggested before. Clark and Curran's (2004) work is in parallelising an implementation of log-linear parsing on the Wall Street Journal Corpus, whereas we focus on part-of-speech tagging of a far larger and more varied web corpus, a technique more widely considered a prerequisite for corpus linguistics research. Curran (2003) suggested distributed processing in terms of web services but only to "allow components developed by different researchers in different locations to be composed to build larger systems" and not for parallel processing. Most significantly, previous investigations have not examined three essential questions: how to apply distributed techniques to vast quantities of corpus data derived from the web, how to ensure that web-derived corpora are representative, and how to provide verifiability and replicability. These core foci of our work represent crucial innovations lacking in prior research. In particular, representativeness and replicability are key research concerns to enhance the reliability of web data for corpora.

In the areas of Natural Language Processing (NLP) and computational linguistics, proposals have been made for using the computational Grid for data-intensive NLP and text-mining for e-Science (Carroll et al., 2005; Hughes et al, 2004). While such an approach promises much in terms of emerging infrastructure, we wish to exploit existing computing infrastructure that is more accessible to linguists via a P2P approach. In simple terms, P2P is a technology that takes advantage of the resources and services available at the edge of the Internet (Shirky, 2001). Better known for file-sharing and Instant Messenger applications, P2P has increasingly been applied in distributed computational systems. Examples include *SETI@home* (looking for radio evidence of extraterrestrial life), *ClimatePrediction.net* (studying climate change), *Predictor@home* (investigating protein-related diseases) and *Einstein@home* (searching for gravitational signals).

A key advantage of P2P systems is that they are lightweight and geared to personal computing where informal groups provide unused processing power to solve a common problem. Typically, P2P systems draw upon the resources that already exist on a network (e.g. home or work PCs), thus keeping the cost to resource ratio low. For example the fastest supercomputer cost over \$110 million to develop and has a peak performance of 12.3 TFLOPS (trillions of floating-point operations per second). In contrast, a typical day for the SETI@home project involved a performance of over 20 TFLOPS, yet cost only \$700,000 to develop; processing power is donated by user PCs. This high yield for low start-up cost makes it ideal for cheaply developing effective computational systems to realise, deploy and evaluate our framework. The deployment of computational based P2P systems is supported by archi-

[9] http://pie.usna.edu/

tectures such as BOINC[10], which provide a platform on which volunteer based distributed computing systems can be built. Lancaster's own P2P Application Framework (Walkerdine et al., submitted) also supports higher-level P2P application development and can be adapted to make use of the BOINC architecture.

3 Research hypothesis and aims

Our research hypothesis is that distributed computational techniques can alleviate the annotation bottleneck for processing corpus data from the web. This leads us to a number of research questions:

- How can corpus data from the web be divided into units for processing via distributed techniques?
- Which corpus annotation techniques are suitable for distributed processing?
- Can distributed techniques assist in corpus clean-up and conversion to allow inclusion of a wider variety of genres and to support more representative corpora?

In the early stages of our proposed research, we are focussing on grammatical word-class analysis (part-of-speech tagging) of web-derived corpora of English and aspects of corpus clean-up and conversion. Clarifying copyright issues and exploring models for legal dissemination of corpora compiled from web data are key objectives of this stage of the investigation as well.

4 Methodology

The initial focus of the work will be to develop the framework for distributed corpus annotation. Since existing solutions have been centralised in nature, we first must examine the consequences that a distributed approach has for corpus annotation and identify issues to address.

A key concern will be handling web pages within the framework, as it is essential to minimise the amount of data communicated between peers. Unlike the other distributed analytical systems mentioned above, the size of text document and analysis time is largely proportional for corpora annotation. This places limitations on work unit size and distribution strategies. In particular, three areas will be investigated:

- *Mechanisms for crawling/discovery of a web corpus domain* - how to identify pages to include in a web corpus. Also investigate appropriate criteria for handling pages which are created or modified dynamically.
- *Mechanisms to generate work units for distributed computation* - how to split the corpus into work units and reduce the communication / computation time ratio that is crucial for such systems to be effective.
- *Mechanisms to support the distribution of work units and collection of results* - how to handle load balancing. What data should be sent to peers and how is the processed information handled and manipulated? What mechanisms should be in place to ensure correctness of results? How can abuse be prevented and security concerns of collaborating institutions be addressed? BOINC already provides a good platform for this, and these aspects will be investigated within the project.

Analysis of existing distributed computation systems will help to inform the design of the framework and tackle some of these issues. Finally, the framework will also cater for three common strategies for corpus annotation:

- *Site based corpus annotation* - in which the user can specify a web site to annotate
- *Domain based corpus annotation* - in which the user specifies a content domain (with the use of keywords) to annotate
- *Crawler based corpus annotation* - more general web based corpus annotation in which crawlers are used to locate web pages

From a computational linguistic view, the framework will also need to take into account the granularity of the unit (for example, POS tagging requires sentence-units, but anaphoric annotation needs paragraphs or larger). Secondly, we need to investigate techniques for identifying identical documents, virtually identical documents and highly repetitive documents, such as those pioneered by Fletcher (2004b) and shingling techniques described by Chakrabarti (2002).

The second stage of our work will involve implementing the framework within a P2P environment. We have already developed a prototype of an object-oriented application environment to support P2P system development using JXTA (Sun's P2P API). We have designed this environment so that specific application functionality

[10] BOINC, Berkeley Open Infrastructure for Network Computing. http://boinc.berkeley.edu.

can be captured within *plug-ins* that can then integrate with the environment and utilise its functionality. This system has been successfully tested with the development of plug-ins supporting instant messaging, distributed video encoding (Hughes and Walkerdine, 2005), distributed virtual worlds (Hughes et al., 2005) and digital library management (Walkerdine and Rayson, 2004). It is our intention to implement our distributed corpus annotation framework as a plug-in. This will involve implementing new functionality and integrating this with our existing annotation tools (such as CLAWS[11]). The development environment is also flexible enough to utilise the BOINC platform, and such support will be built into it.

Using the P2P Application Framework as a basis for the development secures several advantages. First, it reduces development time by allowing the developer to reuse existing functionality; secondly, it already supports essential aspects such as system security; and thirdly, it has already been used successfully to deploy comparable P2P applications. A lightweight version of the application framework will be bundled with the corpus annotation plug-in, and this will then be made publicly available for download in open-source and executable formats. We envisage our end-users will come from a variety of disciplines such as language engineering and linguistics. For the less-technical users, the prototype will be packaged as a screensaver or instant messaging client to facilitate deployment.

5 Evaluation

We will evaluate the framework and prototype developed by applying it as a pre-processor step for the Sketch Engine system. The Sketch Engine requires a large well-balanced corpus which has been part-of-speech tagged and shallow parsed to find subjects, objects, heads, and modifiers. We will use the existing non-distributed processing tools on the Sketch Engine as a baseline for a comparative evaluation of the AWAC framework instantiation by utilising processing power and bandwidth in learning labs at Lancaster University and USNA during off hours.

We will explore techniques to make the resulting annotated web corpus data available in static form to enable replication and verification of corpus studies based on such data. The initial solution will be to store the resulting reference corpus in the Sketch Engine. We will also investigate whether the distributed environment underlying our approach offers a solution to the problem of reproducibility in web-based corpus studies based in general. Current practise elsewhere includes the distribution of URL lists, but given the dynamic nature of the web, this is not sufficiently robust. Other solutions such as complete caching of the corpora are not typically adopted due to legal concerns over copyright and redistribution of web data, issues considered at length by Fletcher (2004a). Other requirements for reference corpora such as retrieval and storage of metadata for web pages are beyond the scope of what we propose here.

To improve the representative nature of web-derived corpora, we will research techniques to enable the importing of additional document types such as PDF. We will reuse and extend techniques implemented in the collection, encoding and annotation of the PERC Corpus of Professional English[12]. A majority of this corpus has been collected by conversion of on-line academic journal articles from PDF to XML with a combination of semi-automatic tools and techniques (including Adobe Acrobat version 6). Basic issues such as character encoding, table/figure extraction and maintaining text flow around embedded images need to be dealt with before annotation processing can begin. We will comparatively evaluate our techniques against others such as pdf2txt, and Multivalent PDF ExtractText[13]. Part of the evaluation will be to collect and annotate a sample corpus. We aim to collect a corpus from the web that is comparable to the BNC in content and annotation. This corpus will be tagged using the P2P framework. It will form a test-bed for the framework and we will utilise the non-distributed annotation system on the Sketch Engine as a baseline for comparison and evaluation. To evaluate text conversion and clean-up routines for PDF documents, we will use a 5-million-word gold-standard sub-corpus extracted

[11] http://www.comp.lancs.ac.uk/ucrel/claws/

[12] The Corpus of Professional English (CPE) is a major research project of PERC (the Professional English Research Consortium) currently underway that, when finished, will consist of a 100-million-word computerised database of English used by professionals in science, engineering, technology and other fields. Lancaster University and Shogakukan Inc. are PERC Member Institutions. For more details, see http://www.perc21.org/

[13] http://multivalent.sourceforge.net/

from the PERC Corpus of Professional English[14].

6 Conclusion

Future work includes an analysis of the balance between computational and bandwidth requirements. It is essential in distributing the corpus annotation to achieve small amounts of data transmission in return for large computational gains for each work-unit.

In this paper, we have discussed the requirement for annotation of web-derived corpus data. Currently, a bottleneck exists in the tagging of web-derived corpus data due to the voluminous amount of corpus processing involved. Our proposal is to construct a framework for large-scale distributed corpus annotation using existing peer-to-peer technology. We have presented the challenges that lie ahead for such an approach. Work is now underway to address the clean-up of PDF data for inclusion into corpora downloaded from the web.

Acknowledgements

We wish to thank the anonymous reviewers who commented our paper. We are grateful to Shogakukan Inc. (Tokyo, Japan) for supporting research at Lancaster University into the process of conversion and clean-up of PDF to text, and to the Professional English Research Consortium for the provision of the gold-standard corpus for our evaluation.

References

Baroni, M. and Bernardini, S. (2004). BootCaT: Bootstrapping Corpora and Terms from the Web. In *Proceedings of LREC2004*, Lisbon, pp. 1313-1316.

Baroni, M. and Sharoff, S. (2005). Creating specialized and general corpora using automated search engine queries. *Web as Corpus Workshop*, Birmingham University, UK, 14th July 2005.

Carroll, J., R. Evans and E. Klein (2005) Supporting text mining for e-Science: the challenges for Grid-enabled natural language processing. In *Workshop on Text Mining, e-Research And Grid-enabled Language Technology at the Fourth UK e-Science Programme All Hands Meeting (AHM2005)*, Nottingham, UK.

Chakrabarti, S. (2002) *Mining the Web: Discovering Knowledge from Hypertext Data*. Morgan Kaufmann.

Clark, S. and Curran, J. R.. (2004). Parsing the wsj using ccg and log-linear models. In *Proceedings of the 42nd Annual Meeting of the Association for Computational Linguistics (ACL '04)*.

Corley, S., Corley, M., Keller, F., Crocker, M., & Trewin, S. (2001). Finding Syntactic Structure in Unparsed Corpora: The Gsearch Corpus Query System. *Computers and the Humanities*, 35, 81-94.

Curran, J.R. (2003). Blueprint for a High Performance NLP Infrastructure. In *Proc. of Workshop on Software Engineering and Architecture of Language Technology Systems (SEALTS)* Edmonton, Canada, 2003, pp. 40 – 45.

Edmonds, P and Kilgarriff, A. (2002). Introduction to the special issue on evaluating word sense disambiguation systems. *Journal of Natural Language Engineering*, 8 (2), pp. 279-291.

Fletcher, W. H. (2001). Concordancing the Web with KWiCFinder. *Third North American Symposium on Corpus Linguistics and Language Teaching*, Boston, MA, 23-25 March 2001.

Fletcher, W. H. (2004a). Facilitating the compilation and dissemination of ad-hoc Web corpora. In G. Aston, S. Bernardini and D. Stewart (eds.), *Corpora and Language Learners*, pp. 271 – 300, John Benjamins, Amsterdam.

Fletcher, W. H. (2004b). Making the Web More Useful as a Source for Linguistic Corpora. In Ulla Connor and Thomas A. Upton (eds.) *Applied Corpus Linguistics. A Multidimensional Perspective*. Rodopi, Amsterdam, pp. 191 – 205.

Granger, S., and Rayson, P. (1998). Automatic profiling of learner texts. In S. Granger (ed.) *Learner English on Computer*. Longman, London and New York, pp. 119-131.

Hughes, B, Bird, S., Haejoong, K., and Klein, E. (2004). Experiments with data-intensive NLP on a computational grid. Proceedings of the International Workshop on Human Language Technology. http://eprints.unimelb.edu.au/archive/00000503/.

Hughes, D., Gilleade, K., Walkerdine, J. and Mariani, J., Exploiting P2P in the Creation of Game Worlds. In the proceedings of ACM GDTW 2005, Liverpool, UK, 8th-9th November, 2005.

Hughes, D. and Walkerdine, J. (2005), Distributed Video Encoding Over A Peer-to-Peer Network. In the *proceedings of PREP 2005*, Lancaster, UK, 30th March - 1st April, 2005

Kehoe, A. and Renouf, A. (2002) WebCorp: Applying the Web to Linguistics and Linguistics to the Web.

[14] This corpus has already been manually re-typed at Shogakukan Inc. from PDF originals downloaded from the web.

World Wide Web 2002 Conference, Honolulu, Hawaii.

Keller, F., Lapata, M. and Ourioupina, O. (2002). Using the Web to Overcome Data Sparseness. *Proceedings of the Conference on Empirical Methods in Natural Language Processing, Philadelphia, July 2002*, pp. 230-237.

Kennedy, G. (1998). *An introduction to corpus linguistics*. Longman, London.

Kilgarriff, A. (2001). Web as corpus. In *Proceedings of Corpus Linguistics 2001*, Lancaster University, 29 March - 2 April 2001, pp. 342 – 344.

Kilgarriff, A. (2003). Linguistic Search Engine. In *proceedings of Workshop on Shallow Processing of Large Corpora (SProLaC 2003)*, Lancaster University, 28 - 31 March 2003, pp. 53 – 58.

Kilgarriff, A. and Grefenstette, G (2003). Introduction to the Special Issue on the Web as Corpus. *Computational Linguistics*, 29: 3, pp. 333-347.

Mair, C. (2005). The corpus-based study of language change in progress: The extra value of tagged corpora. *Presentation at the AAACL/ICAME Conference*, Ann Arbor, May 2005.

Resnik, P. and Elkiss, A. (2003) The Linguist's Search Engine: Getting Started Guide. *Technical Report: LAMP-TR-108/CS-TR-4541/UMIACS-TR-2003-109, University of Maryland*, College Park, November 2003.

Robb, T. (2003) Google as a Corpus Tool? In *ETJ Journal*, Volume 4, number 1, Spring 2003.

Rundell, M. (2000). "The biggest corpus of all", *Humanising Language Teaching*. 2:3; May 2000.

Shirky, C. (2001) Listening to Napster, in Peer-to-Peer: Harnessing the power of Disruptive Technologies, O'Reilly.

Turney, P. (2001). Word Sense Disambiguation by Web Mining for Word Co-occurrence Probabilities. In *proceedings of SENSEVAL-3*, Barcelona, Spain, July 2004 pp. 239-242.

Veronis, J. (2005). Web: Google's missing pages: mystery solved? http://aixtal.blogspot.com/2005/02/web-googles-missing-pages-mystery.html (accessed April 28, 2005).

Walkerdine, J., Gilleade, K., Hughes, D., Rayson, P., Simms, J., Mariani, J., and Sommerville, I. A Framework for P2P Application Development. *Paper submitted to Software Practice and Experience*.

Walkerdine, J. and Rayson, P. (2004) P2P-4-DL: Digital Library over Peer-to-Peer. In Caronni G., Weiler N., Shahmehri N. (eds.) *Proceedings of Fourth IEEE International Conference on Peer-to-Peer Computing (PSP2004)* 25-27 August 2004, Zurich, Switzerland. IEEE Computer Society Press, pp. 264-265.

Web Coverage of the 2004 US Presidential Election

Arno Scharl
Know-Center & Graz
University of Technology
Graz, Austria
scharl@ecoresearch.net

Albert Weichselbraun
Vienna University of Economics and
Business Administration
Vienna, Austria
weichselbraun@ecoresearch.net

Abstract

When corporations, news media and advocacy organizations embrace networked information technology, intentionally or unintentionally, they influence democratic processes. To capture and understand the influence of publicly available electronic content, the US Election 2004 Web Monitor[1] tracked the online coverage of US presidential candidates, and investigated how this coverage reflected their position on environmental issues.

1 Introduction

Most attempts to monitor the campaign performance of presidential candidates focus on public opinion, which is influenced by the consumption of media products. Analyzing patterns of political communication, however, should include the consumption as well as the production of content (Howard 2003). Monitoring candidates' coverage on the Web provides a complementary source of empirical data and window into the evolving concept of electronic democracy (Dutton, Elberse et al. 1999).

A recent *Pew/Internet* survey (Horrigan, Garrett et al. 2004) found that four out of ten US Internet users aged 18 or older accessed political material during the 2004 presidential campaign, up 50 percent from the 2000 campaign. For political news in general, more than two thirds of American broadband users and over half the dial-up users seek Web sites of national news organizations. International news sites are the second most popular category at 24 and 14 percent, respectively.

As traditional media extend their dominant position to the online world, analyzing their Web sites should therefore reflect the majority of political content accessed by the average user.

2 Impact of New Media on Public Opinion

Representative democracy offers significant possibilities for exploiting information networks (Holmes 2002), but there is little agreement on their specific impact. Proponents praise the networks' potential to increase the accessibility of information, encourage participatory decision-making, and facilitate communication with policy officials and like-minded citizens. From an advocate's perspective, disseminating environmental information via the Internet, directly or through news media, creates awareness by emphasizing the interdependency of ecological, economic, and social issues (Scharl 2004).

Critics portray McLuhan's global village as a "neofeudal manor with highly fortified and opulent castles (centers of industrial, financial, and media power) surrounded by vast hinterlands of working peasants clamoring for survival and recognition" (Tehranian 1999, p55f.). They argue that information networks polarize society by linking groups with similar political views. Low-overhead forms of personal publishing (Gruhl, Guha et al. 2004) such as Web logs and online discussion forums, for example, might reinforce a group's world view and shun opposing opinions. This reinforcement, amplified by biased media coverage, polarizes groups (Sunstein 2004) and degrades the climate of public discourse (Horrigan, Garrett et al. 2004).

The communication strategies of news media, corporations and advocacy organizations affect democratic processes. Yet they only condition, rather than determine these processes. Assuming

[1] http://www.ecoresearch.net/election2004

deterministic effects of information networks neglects the world's ambivalence, and results in conflicting claims regarding the networks' political impact. News media are free to choose which candidate to emphasize, and how to interpret current events (Wayne 2001). Most Americans prefer unbiased news sources (Horrigan, Garrett et al. 2004), but Web sites tend to reflect their owners' political agenda, and thus contribute to a polarized electorate.

While a narrow margin decided the last two US presidential elections, differences in the candidates' positions became more pronounced in 2004, and the political deliberation more partisan. Partisans tend to perceive mass media content as biased against their point of view. Explanations for this *hostile media effect* range from selective recall (preferentially remembering hostile content), selective categorization (perceiving the same content differently) and conflicting standards (considering hostile content as invalid or irrelevant). Recent research suggests that selective categorization best explains hostile media effects (Schmitt, Gunther et al. 2004).

3 Methodology

Given an increasingly polarized electorate and hostile media effects that impair partisans' judgment, analyzing political Web content requires objective measures of organizational bias. Yet the volume and dynamic nature of Web documents complicate testing the assumption of organizational bias. To address this challenge, the *US Election 2004 Web Monitor* sampled 1,153 Web sites in weekly intervals. The project drew upon the *Newslink.org*, *Kidon.com* and *ABYZ-NewsLinks.com* directories to compile a list of 42 US news organizations and 72 international sites from four other English-speaking countries: Canada, United Kingdom, Australia and New Zealand. To extend the study, the sample included the Web sites of the Fortune 1000 (the largest US corporations ranked by revenue) and 39 environmental organizations.

Considering the dynamics of Web content in general and presidential campaigns in particular (Howard 2003), a crawling agent mirrored these Web sites by following their hierarchical structure until reaching 50 megabytes of textual data for news media, and 10 megabytes for commercial and advocacy sites. These limits help compare sites of heterogeneous size, and reduce the dilution of top-level information by content in lower hierarchical levels (Scharl 2000).

Such a collection of recorded content used for descriptive analysis is often referred to as corpus. This research investigated and visualized regularities in three groups of Web sites by applying methods from corpus linguistics and textual statistics (Biber, Conrad et al. 1998; Lebart, Salem et al. 1998; McEnery and Wilson 2001).

Quantitative textual analysis of Web documents necessitates three steps in order to yield a useful machine-readable representation (Lebart, Salem et al. 1998):

- The first step *converts* hypertext documents into plain text – i.e., processing the gathered data and eliminating markup code and scripting elements.
- The second step *segments* the textual chain into minimal units by removing coding ambiguities such as punctuation marks, the case of letters, hyphens, or points in abbreviations. In the case of the Election Monitor, this process yielded about half a million documents each week, comprising about 125 million words in 10 million sentences. The system then identified and removed redundant segments such as headlines and news summaries, whose appearance on multiple pages distorts frequency counts.
- The third step, *identification*, groups identical units and counts their occurrences – i.e., creating an inventory of words, or multiword units of meaning (Danielsson 2004). The frequency of candidate references presented in the following section is based on such an exhaustive index, which often uses decreasing frequency of occurrence as the primary sorting criterion and lexicographic order as the secondary criterion.

Frequency of References (Attention)

Media coverage and public recognition go hand-in hand (Wayne 2001), documented by strong correlations between the attention of news media and both public salience and attitudes toward presidential candidates (Kiousis and McCombs 2004). The *US Election 2004 Web Monitor* calculated attention as the relative number of references to a candidate. To determine references to candidates or environmental topics, a pattern matching algorithm considered common term inflections while excluding ambiguous expressions. Only identifying occurrences of *george w. bush*, for example, ignores equally valid references to *president bush* and *george walker bush*.

Figure 1. US Election 2004 Web Monitor one day after the election (Nov 3, 2004)

Yet a general query for *bush* fails to distinguish the president's last name from references to wilderness areas or woody perennial plants.

After the election, nearly two thirds of the media references mentioned George W. Bush and Dick Cheney, up four percentage points from the preceding week (Figure 1). About one third reported on John Kerry and John Edwards. The Fortune 1000 companies and environmental organizations dedicated over 80 percent of their coverage to the president and his running mate.

Across all three samples, the independent team of Ralph Nader and Peter Camejo garnered less than five percent of the attention.

4 Semantic Orientation of References (Attitude)

Calculating the frequency of candidate references disregards their context (Yi, Nasukawa et al. 2003). Therefore, the system also tracked attitude, the semantic orientation of a sentence towards the candidates (Scharl, Pollach et al. 2003).

The algorithm calculated the distance between the target word and 4,400 positive and negative words from the General Inquirer's tagged dictionary (Stone, Dunphy et al. 1966). Reverse lemmatization added about 3,000 terms to the dictionary by considering plurals, gerund forms, past tense suffixes and other syntactical variations (e.g. manipulate → manipulates, manipulating, manipulated).

Two sentences from news media on November 4 exemplify positive vs. negative coverage of a topic (zero indicates neutral coverage). The underlined words, identified in the tagged dictionary, were used to compute the semantic orientation of sentences with oil price references.

- "US stocks <u>rallied</u> Wednesday, <u>boosted</u> by <u>shares</u> of health and <u>defence</u> <u>companies</u> that are seen <u>benefiting</u> from the re-election of President *George W. Bush*, but higher **oil prices** checked <u>advances</u>" (NEW ZEALAND HERALD). ↑ (+ 4.09)
- "The dollar <u>hit</u> its <u>lowest</u> level in more than eight months against the Euro Thursday, <u>falling</u> sharply on <u>worries</u> about the economic effects of rising **oil prices** and expectations of continued trade and budget <u>deficits</u> in *President Bush's* second term" (ST. PETERSBURG TIMES). ↓ (– 4.03)

Initially, media coverage favored the Republicans, although the Democratic contenders gained ground in September 2004 (Figure 2). Kerry's performance in the first televised debate accelerated these gains in media attitude, followed by a tight race between the two teams in the four weeks preceding the election. The re-election of George W. Bush again widened the gap, understandably considering the positive connotation of terms such as *winning* and *victory*.

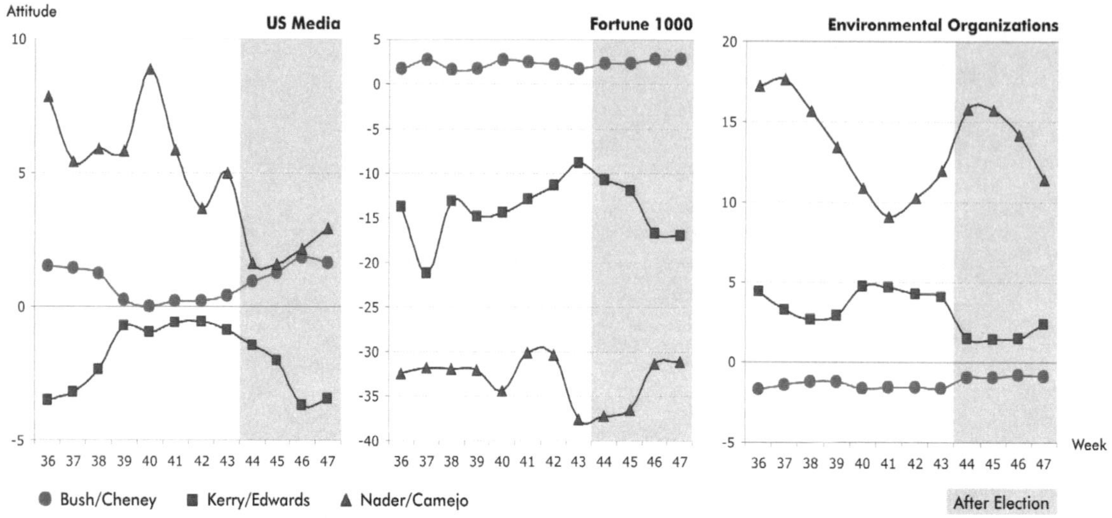

Figure 2. Attitude of the US Media, the Fortune 1000 and environmental organizations towards the US presidential candidates between September and November 2004

Compared to the news media, the other two samples showed more bias. Fortune 1000 companies presented the Republican candidates most favorably, while environmental organizations tended to criticize the environmental record of George W. Bush – particularly abandoning the Kyoto Treaty ratification, and reducing air pollution controls through the Clear Skies Act.

To investigate these claims, separate analyses related environmental issues to Web sites and candidates. In terms of energy policy, for example, one such analysis investigated Web coverage of renewable energy, fossil fuels and nuclear power – a crucial aspect in light of recent geopolitical events and the global environmental impact of US energy policy decisions. On a micro level, the Election Monitor's Web site allowed users to list sentences containing both candidate references and energy-related terms, and sort these sentences by semantic orientation.

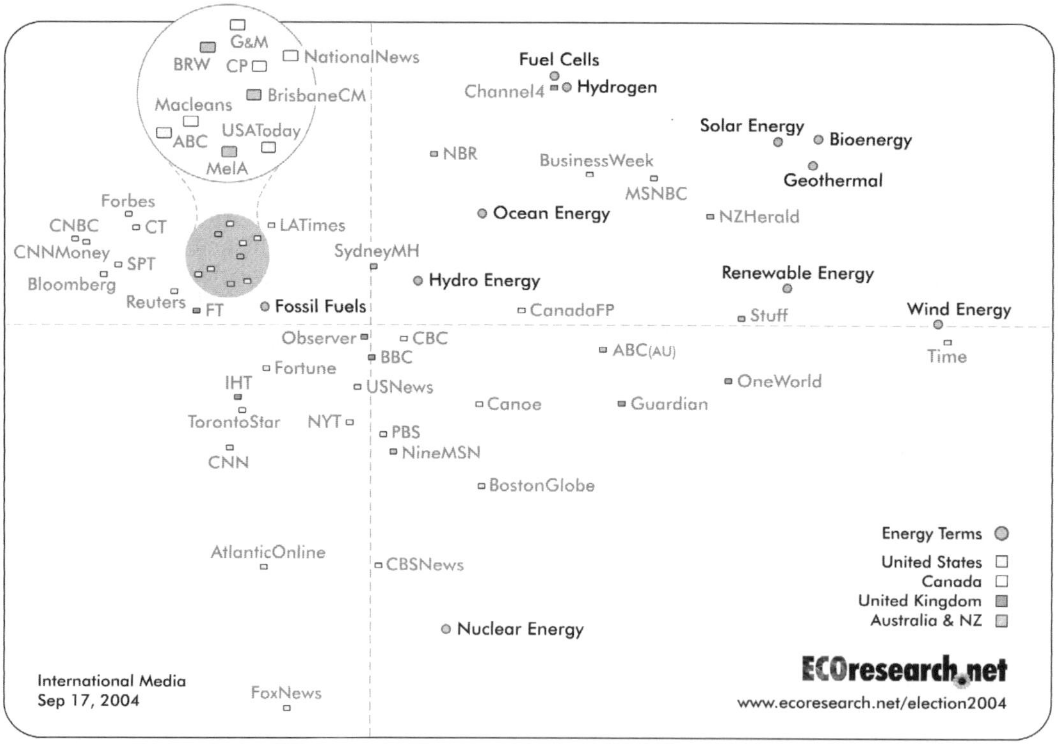

Figure 3. Perceptual map of energy terms among international news media

On a macro level, the perceptual map of Figure 3 summarizes the prominence of energy terms among international media sites. The diagram is based on correspondence analysis, which processed the table of term frequencies as of 17 September 2004. Related concepts and organizations appear close to each other in the computationally created two-dimensional space. The circular and rectangular markers represent energy-related concepts and media sites, respectively. When interpreting the diagram it is important to note that term frequency, not media attitude, determines the position of data points.

The distribution of data points shows a tripolar structure: fossil fuels in the upper left, renewable energies in the upper right, and nuclear energy near the bottom of the diagram. The diagram illustrates news organizations with distinct content – Fox News and Time, for example, with their coverage of *nuclear energy* and *wind energy*, respectively. Geographic differences are also apparent. *Fossil fuels* align with many Australian media, reflecting the country's richness in mineral resources. Most business publications congregate around fossil fuels as well, Business Week being a notable exception.

References to *fuel cells* and *hydrogen* often appear together. Their potential use with various energy sources explains their slightly isolated position. Combining the energy carrier hydrogen with fuel cell conversion technology yields high efficiency and low pollution in applications such as zero-emission vehicles, energy storage and portable electronics.

5 Refining Attitude Measures

Lexically identical occurrences with differing or even opposite meanings, depending on the context, represent an inherent problem of automatically determining the semantic orientation of Web content (Wilson, Wiebe et al. 2005). Word-sense ambiguity, for example, is a common phenomenon. *Arrest* as a noun takes custody by legal authority, for example, while *arrest* as a verb could mean to catch or to stop. Similarly, in economics the noun *good* refers to physical objects or services. As an adjective, *good* assigns desirable or positive qualities. Part of speech tagging considers this variability by annotating Web content and distinguishing between nouns, verbs, adjectives and other parts of speech.

Besides differences in word-sense, analysts also encounter other types of ambiguities – e.g., idiomatic versus non-idiomatic term usage, or various pragmatic ambiguities involving irony, sarcasm, and metaphor (Wiebe, Wilson et al. 2005).

Given the considerable size of the corpus and the need to publish results in weekly intervals, the system was designed to maximize throughput in terms of documents per second. A comparably simple approach restricted to single words and without sentence parsing ensured the timely completion of the weekly calculations.

Planned extensions will add multiple-word combinations to the tagged dictionary to discern morphologically similar but semantically different terms such as *fuel cell* and *prison cell*. Yet the lexis of Web content only partially determines its semantic orientation, despite using multi-word units of meaning instead of single words or lemmas (Danielsson 2004). Prototypical implementations such as the *OpinionFinder* (Wilson, Hoffmann et al. 2005) have demonstrated that grammatical parsing can successfully address this limitation by identifying ambiguities and capturing meaning-making processes at levels beyond lexis – correctly identifying, annotating and evaluating nested expressions of various complexity (Wiebe, Wilson et al. 2005).

6 Keyword Analysis

Keyword Analysis locates words in a given text and compares their frequency with a reference distribution from a usually larger corpus of text. To complement measures of attention and attitude towards a candidate, keywords grouped by political party and geographic region highlighted issues associated with each candidate. For that purpose, the system compared the term frequencies in sentences mentioning a candidate (target corpus) with the term frequencies in the entire sample of 1,153 Web sites from media organizations, the Fortune 1000, and environmental organizations (reference corpus).

The results suggest that personalities and campaign events dominate over substantive policy issues, a possible reason for the average voter's limited interest in and knowledge about political processes (Wayne 2001). Table 1 summarizes keywords that US news media associated with the presidential candidates and their running mates in the week preceding the election. The list ranks keywords by decreasing significance, computed via a chi-square test with Yates' correction for continuity. To avoid outliers, the list only considers nouns with at least 100 occurrences in the reference corpus.

Republicans		Democrats		Independents	
George Bush	**Dick Cheney**	**John Kerry**	**John Edwards**	**Ralph Nader**	**Peter Camejo**
debate	lynne	nominee	carolina	ballot	opinion
challenger	daughter	vietnam	running	percent	running
iraq	halliburton	challenger	debate	candidacy	respondents
gore	debate	debate	nominee	advocate	electors
war	lesbian	massachusetts	gephardt	party	commonwealth
speech	rumsfeld	nomination	iowa	supreme	ballot
nominee	pensacola	war	ashton	gore	endorsement
guard	rally	rival	optimism	petition	nominee
hussein	wyoming	speech	north	court	battleground
terrorism	wilmington	clinton	trail	pennsylvania	balance

Table 1. Keywords of US news media (Oct 27, 2004)

The keywords document that the television *debates* between the major candidates and their *running* mates remained topical up until the election. The *war* on *terrorism* and persistent problems in dealing with insurgents in *Iraq* dogged Bush, while his *challenger's* service in *Vietnam* continued to occupy the media.

Vice-President and former CEO of *Halliburton* Cheney was busy, traveling to *Pensacola, Wyoming* and *Wilmington* and addressing media questions about his wife *Lynne* and his *lesbian* daughter Mary. A *speech* of former President *Clinton,* joining Kerry in his first appearance after undergoing heart surgery, reminded undecided voters of more prosperous times. At the same time, actor *Ashton* Kutcher hit the campaign *trail* for John Edwards, senator from *North Carolina* and *running* mate of John Kerry.

Although the *Supreme Court* refused his *candidacy* in *Pennsylvania* over invalid nominating petitions, Ralph Nader was on the ballot in more than 30 states. Articles about him reiterated controversies over vote-splitting in the previous election, and the *Supreme Court's* decision to end the Bush vs. *Gore* recounts in December 2000.

7 Conclusion and Future Research

The *US Election 2004 Web Monitor* provided a weekly snapshot of international Web coverage, measuring attention and attitude towards the US presidential candidates. Keywords grouped by political party and geographic region summarize issues associated with each candidate.

Compared to the Web sites of news media, campaign managers have less control of spin and impact in media that rely on citizenry for message turnover (Howard 2003). Extending the current system will allow measuring information propagation, not only among corporate Web sites but also via Web logs, online discussion forums and other forms of personal publishing. Investigating the propagation of political content in such environments requires large samples to measure spatial effects, and frequent monitoring to account for temporal effects.

For measuring information propagation, Gruhl et al. (Gruhl, Guha et al. 2004) suggest distinguishing between internally driven, sustained discussions (chatter) and externally induced sharp rises in activity (spikes). Occasionally, spikes result from chatter through resonance when insignificant events trigger massive reactions. Resonance occurs when individual interactions generate large-scale, collective behavior, often showing a sensitive dependence on initial conditions. Social network analysis attempts to explain such macroscopic propagation of information between people, groups and organizations (Kumar, Raghavan et al. 2002). By disseminating information via their social networks, individuals create strong peer influence that often surpasses exogenous influences.

Efforts to create a more responsible electorate (Dutton, Elberse et al. 1999) can leverage this peer influence to trigger self-reinforcing content propagation among individuals. Relationships between these individuals determine the paths of information dissemination. It is along these paths that inter-individual communication multiplies the impact of spikes and creates widespread attention. Knowledge on the structure and determinants of these paths could help promote issue-oriented voting. This in turn would lead to a better-informed electorate aware of its leadership choices, and able to hold decision-makers accountable.

Modeling the production, propagation and consumption of political Web will help address four research questions: How redundant is Web content, and what technical and organizational factors influence information flows within the network? Can existing models of information propagation such as hub-and-spoke, syndication and peer-to-peer adequately explain these information flows? How does Web content influence public opinion, and what are appropriate methods to measure and model the extent, dynamics and latency of this process? Finally, which content placement strategies increase the impact on the target audience and support self-reinforcing propagation among individuals?

Acknowledgements. Our first word of appreciation goes to Jamie Murphy for his ongoing support throughout the project. We would also like to thank Astrid Dickinger, Wilhelm Langenberger, Wei Liu, Antonijo Nikolic, Maya Purushothaman, Dave Webb and Mark Winkler for their valuable help and suggestions. The US Election 2004 Web Monitor represents an initiative of the Research Network on Environmental Online Communication (www.ecoresearch.net), cooperating with the University of Western Australia, Graz University of Technology, Vienna University of Economics and Business Administration, and the Know-Center, which is funded by the Austrian Competence Center program Kplus under the auspices of the Austrian Ministry of Transport, Innovation and Technology (http://www.ffg.at) and by the State of Styria.

References

Biber, D., S. Conrad, et al. (1998). *Corpus Linguistics – Investigating Language Structure and Use.* Cambridge, Cambridge University Press.

Danielsson, P. (2004). "Automatic Extraction of Meaningful Units from Corpora", *International Journal of Corpus Linguistics,* 8(1): 109-127.

Dutton, W. H., A. Elberse, et al. (1999). "A Case Study of a Netizen's Guide to Elections", *Communications of the ACM,* 42(12): 48-54.

Gruhl, D., R. Guha, et al. (2004). Information Diffusion Through Blogspace. *13th International World Wide Web Conference,* New York, USA, ACM Press.

Holmes, N. (2002). "Representative Democracy and the Profession", *Computer,* 35(2): 118-120.

Horrigan, J., K. Garrett, et al. (2004). *The Internet and Democratic Debate.* Washington, Pew Internet & American Life Project.

Howard, P. N. (2003). "Digitizing the Social Contract: Producing American Political Culture in the Age of New Media", *The Communication Review,* 6: 213-245.

Kiousis, S. and M. McCombs (2004). "Agenda-Setting Effects and Attitude Strength – Political Figures during the 1996 Presidential Election", *Communication Research,* 31(1): 36-57.

Kumar, R., P. Raghavan, et al. (2002). "The Web and Social Networks", *Computer,* 35(11): 32-36.

Lebart, L., A. Salem, et al. (1998). *Exploring Textual Data.* Dordrecht, Kluwer Academic Publishers.

McEnery, T. and A. Wilson (2001). *Corpus Linguistics.* Edinburgh, Edinburgh University Press.

Scharl, A. (2000). *Evolutionary Web Development.* London, Springer. http://webdev.wu-wien.ac.at/.

Scharl, A., Ed. (2004). *Environmental Online Communication.* London, Springer. http://www.ecoresearch.net/springer/.

Scharl, A., I. Pollach, et al. (2003). Determining the Semantic Orientation of Web-based Corpora. *Intelligent Data Engineering and Automated Learning, 4th International Conference, IDEAL-2003* (Lecture Notes in Computer Science, Vol. 2690). J. Liu, Y. Cheung and H. Yin. Berlin, Springer: 840-849.

Schmitt, K. M., A. C. Gunther, et al. (2004). "Why Partisans See Mass Media as Biased", *Communication Research,* 31(6): 623-641.

Stone, P. J., D. C. Dunphy, et al. (1966). *The General Inquirer: A Computer Approach to Content Analysis.* Cambridge, MIT Press.

Sunstein, C. R. (2004). "Democracy and Filtering", *Communications of the ACM,* 47(12): 57-59.

Tehranian, M. (1999). *Global Communication and World Politics – Domination, Development, and Discourse.* Boulder, Lynne Rienner.

Wayne, S. J. (2001). *The Road to the White House 2000 – The Politics of Presidential Elections.* New York, Palgrave.

Wiebe, J., T. Wilson, et al. (2005). "Annotating Expressions of Opinions and Emotions in Language", *Language Resources and Evaluation* 39(2-3): 165-210.

Wilson, T., P. Hoffmann, et al. (2005). OpinionFinder – A System for Subjectivity Analysis. *Human Language Technology Conference / Conference on Empirical Methods in Natural Language Processing (HLT-EMNLP 2005),* Vancouver, Canada.

Wilson, T., J. Wiebe, et al. (2005). Recognizing Contextual Polarity in Phrase-Level Sentiment Analysis. *Human Language Technology Conference / Conference on Empirical Methods in Natural Language Processing (HLT-EMNLP 2005),* Vancouver, Canada.

Yi, J., T. Nasukawa, et al. (2003). Sentiment Analyzer: Extracting Sentiments about a Given Topic using Natural Language Processing Techniques. *3rd IEEE International Conference on Data Mining,* Florida, USA.

Corporator: A tool for creating RSS-based specialized corpora

Cédrick Fairon
Centre de traitement automatique du langage
UCLouvain
Belgique
cedrick.fairon@uclouvain.be

Abstract

This paper presents a new approach and a software for collecting specialized corpora on the Web. This approach takes advantage of a very popular XML-based norm used on the Web for sharing content among websites: RSS (Really Simple Syndication). After a brief introduction to RSS, we explain the interest of this type of data sources in the framework of corpus development. Finally, we present Corporator, an Open Source software which was designed for collecting corpus from RSS feeds.

1 Introduction[1]

Over the last years, growing needs in the fields of Corpus Linguistics and NLP have led to an increasing demand for text corpora. The automation of corpus development has therefore became an important and active field of research. Until recently, constructing corpora required large teams and important means (as text was rarely available on electronic support and computer had limited capacities). Today, the situation is quite different as any published text is recorded, at some point of its "life" on digital media. Also, increasing number of electronic publication (textual databank, CD–ROM, etc.) and the expansion of the Internet have made text more accessible than ever in our history.

The Internet is obviously a great source of data for corpus development. It is either considered as a corpus by itself (see the WebCorp Project of Renouf, 2003) or as a huge databank in which to look for specific texts to be selected and gathered for further treatment. Examples of projects adopting the latter approach are numerous (among many Sekigushi and Yammoto, 2004; Emirkanian *et al.* 2004). It is also the goal of the WaCky Project for instance which aims at developing tools "that will allow linguists to crawl a section of the web, process the data, index them and search them"[2].

So we have the Internet: it is immense, free, easily accessible and can be used for all manner of language research (Kilgarriff and Grefenstette, 2003). But text is so abundant, that it is not so easy to find appropriate textual data for a given task. For this reason, researchers have been developing softwares that are able to crawl the Web and find sources corresponding to specific criteria. Using clustering algorithms or similarity measures, it is possible to select texts that are similar to a training set. These techniques can achieve good results, but they are sometimes limited when it comes to distinguishing between well-written texts vs. poorly written, or other subtle criteria. In any case, it will require filtering and cleaning of the data (Berland and Grabar, 2002).

One possibility to address the difficulty to find good sources is to avoid "wide crawling" but instead to bind the crawler to manually identified Web domains which are updated on a regular basis and which offer textual data of good quality (this can be seen as "vertical crawling" as opposed to "horizontal" or "wide crawling"). This is the choice made in the GlossaNet system (Fairon, 1998; 2003). This Web service gives to the users access to a linguistics based search engine for querying online newspapers (it is based on the Open Source corpus processor Unitex[3] – Paumier, 2003). Online newspapers are an interesting source of textual data on the Web because they are continuously updated and they usually publish articles reviewed through a full editorial

[1] I would like to thank CENTAL members who took part in the development and the administration of GlossaNet and those who contributed to the development of Corporator and GlossaRSS. Thanks also to Herlinda Vekemans who helped in the preparation of this paper.

[2] http://wacky.sslmit.unibo.it

[3] http://www-igm.univ-mlv.fr/~unitex/

process which ensures (a certain) quality of the text.

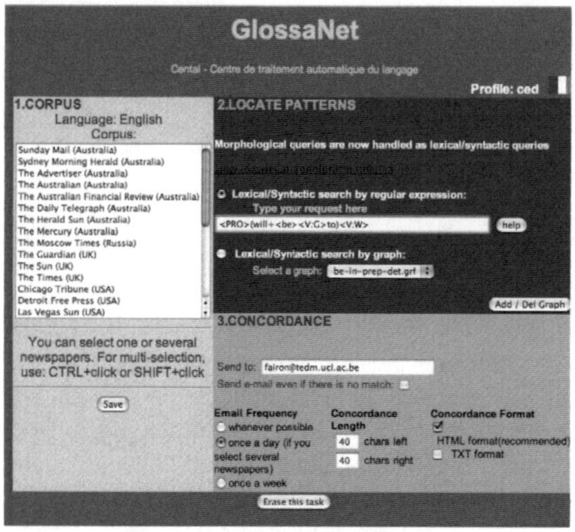

Figure 1. GlossaNet interface

GlossaNet downloads over 100 newspapers (in 10 languages) on a daily basis and parses them like corpora. The Web-based interface[4] of this service enable the user to select a list of newspapers and to register a query. Every day, the user's query is applied on the updated corpus and results are sent by email to the user under the form of a concordance. The main limitation of GlossaNet is that it works only on a limited set of sources which all are of the same kind (newspapers).

In this paper we will present a new approach which takes advantage of a very popular XML-based format used on the Web for sharing content among websites: RSS (Really Simple Syndication). We will briefly explain what RSS is and discuss its possibilities of use for building corpora.

We will also present Corporator, an Open Source program we have developed for creating RSS-fed specialized corpora. This system is not meant to replace broad Web crawling approaches but rather systems like GlossaNet, which collect Web pages from a comparatively small set of homogeneous Web sites.

2 From RSS news feeds to corpora

2.1 What is RSS

RSS is the acronym for *Really Simple Syndication*[5]. It is an XML-based format used for facilitating news publication on the Web and content interchange between websites[6]. Netscape created this standard in 1999, on the basis of Dave Winer's work on the ScriptingNews format (historically the first syndication format used on the Web)[7]. Nowadays many of the press groups around the world offer RSS-based news feeds on their Web sites which allow easy access to the recently published news articles:

FR Le monde :
http://www.lemonde.fr/web/rss/0,48-0,1-0,0.html
IT La Repubblica
http://www.repubblica.it/servizi/rss/index.html
PT Público
http://www.publico.clix.pt/homepage/site/rss/default.asp
US New York Times
http://www.nytimes.com/services/xml/rss/index.html
ES El Pais :
http://www.elpais.es/static/rss/index.html
AF Allafrica.com[8]
http://fr.allafrica.com/tools/headlines/rss.html
etc.

Figure 2. Example of RSS feeds proposed by Reuters (left) and the New York Times (right)

[4] http://glossa.fltr.ucl.ac.be

[5] To be more accurate, 'r' in RSS was initially a reference to RDF. In fact, at the beginning of RSS the aim was to enable automatic Web site summary and at that time, RSS stood for *RDF Site Summary format*. But over the time this standard changed for becoming a news syndication tools and the RDF headers were removed.

[6] Atom is another standard built with the same objective but is more flexible from a technical point of view. For a comparison, see http://www.tbray.org/atom/RSS-and-Atom or Hammersley (2005).

[7] After 99, many groups were involved in the development of RSS and it is finally Harvard which published RSS 2.0 specifications under Creative Commons License in 2003. For further details on the RSS' history, see http://blogs.law.harvard.edu/tech/rssVersionHistory/

[8] AllAfrica gathers and indexes content from more than 125 African press agencies and other sources.

Figure 2 shows two lists of RSS proposed by Reuters and the New York Times respectively. Each link points to a RSS file that contains a list of articles recently published and corresponding to the selected theme or section. RSS files do not contain full articles, but only the title, a brief summary, the date of publication, and a link to the full article available on the publisher Web site. On a regular basis (every hour or even more frequently), RSS documents are updated with fresh content.

News publishers usually organize news feeds by theme (politics, health, business, etc.) and/or in accordance with the various sections of the newspaper (front page, job offers, editorials, regions, etc.). Sometimes they even create feeds for special hot topics such as "Bird flu", in Figure 2 (Reuters).

There is a clear tendency to increase the number of available feeds. We can even say that there is some kind of competition going on as competitors tend to offer more or better services than the others. By proposing accurate feeds of information, content publishers try to increase their chance to see their content reused and published on other websites (see below §2.2). Another indicator of the attention drawn to RSS applications is that some group initiatives are taken for promoting publishers by publicizing their RSS sources. For instance, the French association of online publishers (GESTE[9]) has released an Open Source RSS reader[10] which includes more than 274 French news feeds (among which we can find feeds from *Le Monde, Libération, L'Equipe, ZDNet*, etc.).

2.2 What is RSS?

RSS is particularly well suited for publishing content that can be split into items and that is updated regularly. So it is very convenient for publishing news, but it is not limited to news.

There are two main situations of use for RSS. First, on the user side, people can use an RSS enabled Web client (usually called *news aggregator*) to read news feeds. Standalone applications (like *BottomFeeder*[11] ou *Feedreader*[12]) coexist with plug-ins readers to be added to a regular Web browser. For example, *Wizz RSS News Reader* is an extension for Firefox. It is illustrated in Figure 3: the list of items provided by a RSS is displayed in the left frame. A simple click on one item opens the original article in the right frame.

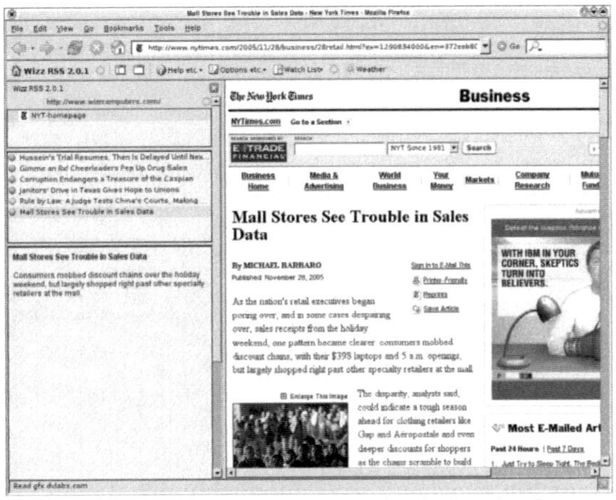

Figure 3. News aggregator plugin in Firefox

Second, on the Web administrator side, this format facilitates the integration in one Web site of content provided by another Web site under the form of a RSS. Thanks to this format, Google can claim to integrate news from 4500 online sources updated every 15 minutes[13].

2.3 How does the XML code looks like?

As can be see in Figure 4[14], the XML-based format of RSS is fairly simple. It mainly consists of a "channel" which contains a list of "items" described by a title, a link, a short description (or summary), a publication date, etc. This example shows only a subset of all the elements (tags) described by the standard[15].

```
<?xml version="1.0" encoding="iso-8859-1" ?>
<rss version="2.0">
  <channel>
    <title>NYT &gt; World Business</title>
      <item>
        <title>Russia and Ukraine Reach Compromise</title>
        <link>http://www.nytimes.com/2006/01/05/05ukraine.html</link>
        <description>The solution allowed both nations...</description>
        <author>ANDREW E. KRAMER</author>
        <pubDate>Thu, 05 Jan 2006 00:00:00 EDT</pubDate>
      </item>
    </title>
  </channel>
</rss>
```

Figure 4: example of RSS feed

2.4 Can RSS feed corpora?

As mentioned above, RSS feeds contain few text. They are mainly a list of items, but each item has a link pointing to the full article. It is therefore

[9] http://www.geste.fr
[10] AlerteInfo, http://www.geste.fr/alertinfo/home.html
[11] http://www.cincomsmalltalk.com/BottomFeeder/
[12] http://www.feedreader.com
[13] http://news.google.com
[14] This example comes from the New York Times "World Business" RSS feed and was simplified to fit our needs.
[15] It is also possible to add elements not described in RSS 2.0 if they are described in a namespace.

easy to create a kind of "greedy" RSS reader which does not only read the feed, but also download each related Web page. This was our goal when we developed Corporator, the program presented in section 3.

2.5 Why using RSS feeds?

The first asset of RSS feeds in the framework of corpus development is that they offer pre-classified documents by theme, genre or other categories. If the classification fits the researcher needs, it can be used for building a specialized corpus. Paquot and Fairon (Forthcoming), for instance, used this approach for creating corpora of editorials in several languages, which can serve as comparable corpora to the ICLE[16] argumentative essays, see section 3.1). Classification is of course extremely interesting for building specialized corpora, but there are two limitations of this asset:

- The classification is not standardized among content publishers. So it will require some work to find equivalent news feeds from different publishers. Figure 2 offers a good illustration of this: the categories proposed by Reuters and the New York Times do not exactly match (even if they both have in common some feeds like *sports* or *science*).
- We do not have a clear view on how the classification is done (manually by the authors, by the system administrators, or even automatically?).

A second asset is that RSS are updated on a regular basis. As such, an RSS feed provides a continuous flow of data that can be easily collected in a corpus. We could call this a *dynamic corpus* (Fairon, 1999) as it will grow over time. We could also use the term *monitor corpus* which was proposed by Renouf (1993) and which is widely used in the Anglo-Saxon community of corpus linguistics.

A third asset is that the quality of the language in one feed will be approximately constant. We know that one of the difficulties when we crawl the Web for finding sources is that we can come across any kind of document of different quality. By selecting "trusted" RSS sources, we can insure an adequate quality of the retrieved texts.

We can also note that RSS feeds comprise the title, date of publication and the author's name of the articles referred to. This is also an advantage because this information can be difficult to extract from HTML code (as it is rarely well structured). As soon as we know the date of publication, we can easily download only up to date information, a task that is not always easy with regular crawlers.

On the side of these general assets, it is also easy to imagine the interest of this type of sources for specific applications such as linguistic survey of the news (neologism identification, term extraction, dictionary update, etc.).

All these advantages would not be very significant if the number of sources was limited. But as we indicated above, the number of news feeds is rapidly and continuously growing, and not only on news portals. Specialized websites are building index of RSS feeds[17] (but we need to remark that for the time being traditional search engines such as Google, MSN, Yahoo, etc. handle RSS feeds poorly). It is possible to find feeds on virtually any domain (cooking, health, sport, education, travels, sciences) and in many languages.

3 Corporator: a "greedy" news agreggator

Corporator[18] is a simple command line program which is able to read an RSS file, find the links in it and download referenced documents. All these HTML documents are filtered and gathered in one file as illustrated in Figure 5.

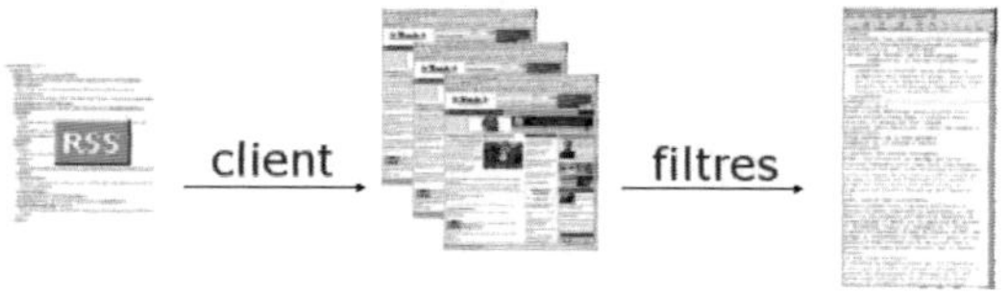

Figure 5. Corporator Process

The filtering step is threefold:

- it removes HTML tags, comments and scripts;
- it removes (as much as possible) the worthless part of the text (text from ads,

[16] See Granger *et al.* (2002).

[17] Here is just a short selection: http://www.newsxs.com, http://www.newsisfree.com, http://www.rss-scout.de, http://www.2rss.com, http://www.lamoooche.com.

[18] Corporator is an Open Source program written in Perl. It was developed on the top of a preexisting Open Sources command line RSS reader named The Yoke. It will be shortly made available on CENTAL's web site: http://cental.fltr.ucl.ac.be.

links, options and menu from the original Web page)[19].

- it converts the filtered text from its original character encoding to UTF8. Corporator can handle the download of news feeds in many languages (and encodings: UTF, latin, iso, etc.)[20].

The program can easily be set up in a task scheduler so that it runs repeatedly to check if new items are available. As long as the task remains scheduled, the corpus will keep on growing.

Figure 6 shows a snapshot of the resulting corpus. Each downloaded news item is preceded by a header that contains information found in the RSS feed.


```
<article>
<source>http://www.nytimes.com/2006/01/03/national/03cnd-mine.html</source>
<date>2006-1-4 / 2:7:49</date>
<title>Rescuers Nearing Trapped Miners, but Air Quality Is Poor...</title>
<description>Rescuers hoped to reach the 13 miners within ...</description>
<text>
Rescuers Nearing Trapped Miners, but Air Quality Is Poor
==========================================================

By JAMES DAO Published: January 3, 2006

SAGO, W.Va., Jan. 3 - Rescuers were within 1,000 to 2,000 feet of where they
believe 13 miners are trapped 260 feet underground and hoped to reach them within
a few hours, the mine's owner said early this evening.

Gov. Joe Manchin III spoke with residents today about rescue operations at the
mine in Sago, W.Va., where 13 workers are trapped.

He said the rescuers were making "significant progress" but that the carbon
monoxide levels remained three times higher than breathable levels, and he
acknowledged that "we are in a situation where we need a miracle."
[...]
</text>
</article>
```


Figure 6. Example or resulting corpus

Corporator is a generic tool, built for downloading any feeds in any language. This goal of genericity comes along with some limitations. For instance, for any item in the RSS feed, the program will download only one Web page even if, on some particular websites, articles can be split over several pages: Reuters[21] for instance splits its longer articles into several pages so that each one can fit on the screen. The RSS news item will only refer to the first page and Corporator will only download that page. It will therefore insert an incomplete article in the corpus. We are still working on this issue.

[19] This is obviously the most difficult step. Several options have been implemented to improve the accuracy of this filter : *delete text above the article title, delete text after pattern X, delete line if matches pattern X, etc.*

[20] It can handle all the encodings supported by the Perl modules Encode (for information, see Encode::Supported on Cpan). Although, experience shows that using the Encode can be complicated.

[21] http://today.reuters.com

3.1 Example of corpus creation

In order to present a first evaluation of the system, we provide in Figure 7 some information about an ongoing corpus development project. Our aim is to build corpora of editorials in several languages, which can serve as comparable corpora to the ICLE argumentative essays (Paquot and Fairon, forthcoming). We have therefore selected "Editorial", "Opinion" and other sections of various newspapers, which are expected to contain argumentative texts. Figure 7 gives for four of these sources the number of articles[22] downloaded between January 1st 2006 and January 31st 2006 (RSS feed names are given between brackets and URLs are listed in the footnotes). Tokens were counted using Unitex (see above) on the filtered text (*i.e.* text already cleaned from HTML and non-valuable text).

Figure 7 shows that the amount of text provided for a given section (here, *Opinion*) by different publishers can be very different. It also illustrates the fact that it is not always possible to find corresponding news feeds among different publishers: *Le Monde*, for instance, does not provide its editorials on a particular news feed. We have therefore selected a rubric named *Rendez-vous* in replacement (we have considered that it contains a text genre of interest to our study).

Le Monde[23] (*Rendez-vous*)
- 58 articles
- 90,208 tokens

New York Times[24] (*Opinion*)
- 220 articles
- 246,104 tokens

Washington Post[25] (*Opinion*)
- 95 articles
- 137,566 tokens

El Pais[26] (*Opinión*)
- 337 articles
- 399,831 tokens

Figure 7. Download statistics: number of articles downloaded in January 2006

[22] This is the number of articles recorded by the program after filtering. It may not correspond exactly to the number of articles really published on this news feed.

[23] www.lemonde.fr/rss/sequence/0,2-3238,1-0,0.xml

[24] www.nytimes.com/services/xml/rss/nyt/Opinion.xml

[25] www.washingtonpost.com/wp-dyn/rss/index.html#opinion

[26] www.elpais.es/rss/feed.html?feedId=1003

3.2 Towards an online service

Linguists may find command line tools hard to use. For this reason, we have also developed a Web-based interface for facilitating RSS-based corpus development. GlossaRSS provides a simple Web interface in which users can create "corpus-acquisition tasks". They just choose a name for the corpus, provide a list of URL corresponding to RSS feeds and activate the download. The corpus will grow automatically over time and the user can at any moment log in to download the latest version of the corpus. For efficiency reasons, the download managing program checks that news feeds are downloaded only once. If several users require the same feed, it will be downloaded once and then appended to each corpus.

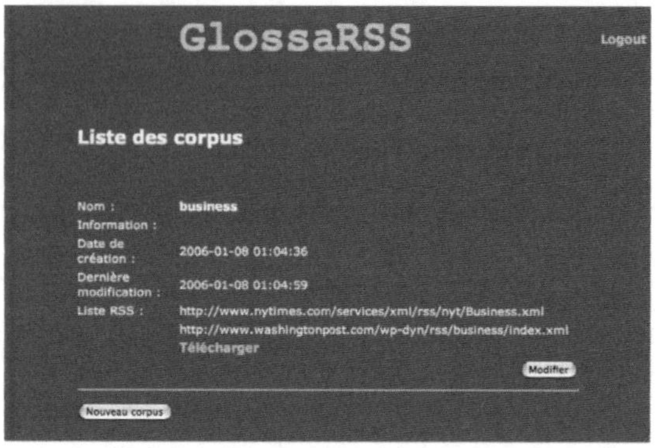

Figure 8. Online service for building RSS-based corpora

This service is being tested and will be made public shortly. Furthermore, we plan to integrate this procedure to GlossaNet. At the moment, GlossaNet provides language specialists with a linguistic search engine that can analyze a little more than 100 newspapers (as seen in Figure 1, users who register a linguistic query can compose a corpus by selecting newspapers in a predefined list). Our goal is to offer the same service in the future but on RSS-based corpora. So it will be possible to create a new corpus, register a linguistic query and get concordance on a daily or weekly basis by email. There is no programming difficulty, but there is a clear issue on the side of "scalability" (at the present time, GlossaNet counts more than 1,300 users and generates more than 18,800 queries a day. The computing charge would probably be difficult to cope with if each user started to build and work on a different corpus). An intermediate approach between the current list of newspapers and an open system would be to define in GlossaNet some thematic corpora that would be fed by RSS from different newspapers.

3.3 From text to RSS-based speech corpora

The approach presented in this paper focuses on text corpora, but could be adapted for collecting speech corpora. In fact RSS are also used as a way for publishing multimedia files through Web feeds named "podcasts". Many medias, corporations or individuals use podcasting for placing audio and video files on the Internet. The advantage of podcast compared with streaming or simple download, is "integration". Users can collect programs from a variety of sources and subscribe to them using a podcast-aware software which will regularly check if new content is available. This technology has been very successful in the last two years and has been rapidly growing in importance. Users have found many reasons to use it, sometimes creatively: language teachers, for example, have found there a very practical source of authentic recordings for their lessons. Regarding corpus development, the interest of podcasting is similar to the ones of text-based RSS (categorization, content regularly updated, etc.). Another interesting fact is that sometimes transcripts are published together with the podcast and it is therefore a great source for creating sound/text corpora[27].

Many portals offer lists of poscast[28]. One of the most interesting ones, is Podzinger[29] which not only indexes podcasts metadata (title, author, date, etc.), but uses a speech recognition system for indexing podcast content.

It would require only minor technical adaptation to enable Corporator to deal with podcasts, something that will be done shortly. Of course, this will only solve the problem of collecting sound files, not the problem of converting these files into speech data useful for linguistic research.

4 Conclusion

Corpora uses and applications are every year more numerous in NLP, language teaching, corpus linguistics, etc. and there is therefore a growing demand for large well-tailored corpora. At the same time the Internet has grown enormously, increasing its diversity and its world

[27] It is even possible to find services that do podcast transcripts (http://castingwords.com).

[28] http://www.podcastingnews.com, http://www.podcast.net, etc.

[29] http://www.podzinger.com

wide coverage. It is now an ideal "ground" for finding corpus sources. But these assets (size, diversity) is at the same time an issue for finding good, reliable, well-written, sources that suit our needs. This is the reason why we need to develop intelligent source-finder crawlers and other softwares specialized in corpus collection. Our contribution to this effort is to bring the researchers' attention to a particularly interesting source of text on the Internet: RSS news feeds. The main interest of this source is to provide classified lists of documents continuously updated and consistent in terms of language quality.

To build specialized corpora with a traditional crawler approach, the process will probably consist in retrieving documents (using a search engine as starting point) and then sorting the retrieved documents and selecting the ones that pass some kind of validity tests. With RSS-based corpus, the approach is different and could be summarized as follows: **do not sort a list of retrieved documents, but retrieve a list of sorted documents**. This is of course only possible if we can find RSS-feeds compatible with the theme and/or language we want in our corpus.

References

Berland, Sophie and Natalia Grabar. 2002. Assistance automatique pour l'homogénéisation d'un corpus Web de spécialité. In *Actes des 6èmes Journées internationales d'analyse statistique des données textuelles (JADT 2002).* Saint-Malo.

Fairon, Cédrick. 1999. Parsing a Web site as a corpus. In C. Fairon (ed.). *Analyse lexicale et syntaxique: Le système INTEX,* Lingvisticae Investigationes Tome XXII (Volume spécial). John Benjamins Publishing, Amsterdam/Philadelphia, pp. 327-340.

Granger, Sylviane, Estelle Dagneaux and Fanny Meunier (eds). 2002. *The International Corpus of Learner English.* CD-ROM and Handbook. Presses universitaires de Louvain, Louvain-la-Neuve.

Hammersley, Ben. 2005. *Developing Feeds with RSS and Atom.* O'Reilly, Sebastopol, CA.

Kilgarriff, Adam and Gregory Grefenstette. 2003. Introduction to the Special Issue on the Web as Corpus. *Computational Linguistics,* Vol. 29(3): 333-348.

Paquot, Magali and Cédrick Fairon. (forthcoming). Investigating L1-induced learner variability: Using the Web as a source of L1 comparable data.

Paumier, Sébastien. 2003. *De la reconnaissance de formes linguistiques à l'analyse syntaxique,* Ph.D., Université de Marne-la-Vallée.

Renouf, Antoinette. 1993. 'A Word in Time: first findings from the investigation of dynamic text'. In J. Aarts, P. de Haan and N. Oostdijk (eds), *English Language Corpora: Design, Analysis and Exploitation,* Rodopi, Amsterdam, pp. 279-288.

Renouf, Antoinette. 2003. 'WebCorp: providing a renewable energy source for corpus linguistics'. In S. Granger and S. Petch-Tyson (eds), *Extending the scope of corpus-based research: new applications, new challenges,* Rodopi , Amsterdam, pp. 39-58.

Sekiguchi, Youichi and Kazuhide Yamamoto. 2004. 'Improving Quality of the Web Corpus'. In *Proceedings of The First International Joint Conference on Natural Language Processing (IJCNLP-04),* pp. 201-206.

Emirkanian Louisette, Christophe Fouqueré and Fabrice Issac. 2004. Corpus issus du Web : analyse des pertinences thématique et informationnelle. In G. Purnelle, C. Fairon and A. Dister (eds), *Le Poids des mots. Actes des 7èmes Journées internationales d'analyse statistique des données textuelles (JADT 2004),* Presses universitaires de Louvain, Louvain-La-Neuve, pp. 390-398.

The problem of ontology alignment on the web: a first report

Davide Fossati and **Gabriele Ghidoni** and **Barbara Di Eugenio**
and **Isabel Cruz** and **Huiyong Xiao** and **Rajen Subba**
Computer Science
University of Illinois
Chicago, IL, USA
dfossa1@uic.edu, red.one.999@virgilio.it, bdieugen@cs.uic.edu
ifc@cs.uic.edu, hxiao2@uic.edu, rsubba@cs.uic.edu

Abstract

This paper presents a general architecture and four algorithms that use Natural Language Processing for automatic ontology matching. The proposed approach is purely instance based, i.e., only the instance documents associated with the nodes of ontologies are taken into account. The four algorithms have been evaluated using real world test data, taken from the Google and LookSmart online directories. The results show that NLP techniques applied to instance documents help the system achieve higher performance.

1 Introduction

Many fundamental issues about the viability and exploitation of the web as a linguistic corpus have not been tackled yet. The web is a massive repository of text and multimedia data. However, there is not a systematic way of classifying and retrieving these documents. Computational Linguists are of course not the only ones looking at these issues; research on the Semantic Web focuses on providing a semantic description of all the resources on the web, resulting into *a mesh of information linked up in such a way as to be easily processable by machines, on a global scale. You can think of it as being an efficient way of representing data on the World Wide Web, or as a globally linked database.*[1] The way the vision of the Semantic Web will be achieved, is by describing each document using languages such as RDF Schema and OWL, which are capable of explicitly expressing the meaning of terms in vocabularies and the relationships between those terms.

The issue we are focusing on in this paper is that these languages are used to define ontologies as well. If ultimately a single ontology were used to describe all the documents on the web, systems would be able to exchange information in a transparent way for the end user. The availability of such a standard ontology would be extremely helpful to NLP as well, e.g., it would make it far easier to retrieve all documents on a certain topic. However, until this vision becomes a reality, a plurality of ontologies are being used to describe documents and their content. The task of *automatic ontology alignment* or *matching* (Hughes and Ashpole, 2005) then needs to be addressed.

The task of ontology matching has been typically carried out manually or semi-automatically, for example through the use of graphical user interfaces (Noy and Musen, 2000). Previous work has been done to provide automated support to this time consuming task (Rahm and Bernstein, 2001; Cruz and Rajendran, 2003; Doan et al., 2003; Cruz et al., 2004; Subba and Masud, 2004). The various methods can be classified into two main categories: *schema based* and *instance based*. *Schema based* approaches try to infer the semantic mappings by exploiting information related to the structure of the ontologies to be matched, like their topological properties, the labels or description of their nodes, and structural constraints defined on the schemas of the ontologies. These methods do not take into account the actual data classified by the ontologies. On the other hand, *instance based* approaches look at the information contained in the instances of each element of the schema. These methods try to infer the relationships between the nodes of the ontologies from the analysis of their instances. Finally, *hybrid* approaches combine schema and instance based

[1] `http://infomesh.net/2001/swintro/`

methods into integrated systems.

Neither instance level information, nor NLP techniques have been extensively explored in previous work on ontology matching. For example, (Agirre et al., 2000) exploits documents (instances) on the WWW to enrich WordNet (Miller et al., 1990), i.e., to compute "concept signatures," collection of words that significantly distinguish one sense from another, however, not directly for ontology matching. (Liu et al., 2005) uses documents retrieved via queries augmented with, for example, synonyms that WordNet provides to improve the accuracy of the queries themselves, but not for ontology matching. NLP techniques such as POS tagging, or parsing, have been used for ontology matching, but on the names and definitions in the ontology itself, for example, in (Hovy, 2002), hence with a schema based methodology.

In this paper, we describe the results we obtained when using some simple but effective NLP methods to align web ontologies, using an instance based approach. As we will see, our results show that more sophisticated methods do not necessarily lead to better results.

2 General architecture

The instance based approach we propose uses NLP techniques to compute matching scores based on the documents classified under the nodes of ontologies. There is no assumption on the structural properties of the ontologies to be compared: they can be any kind of graph representable in OWL. The instance documents are assumed to be text documents (plain text or HTML).

The matching process starts from a pair of ontologies to be aligned. The two ontologies are traversed and, for each node having at least one instance, the system computes a *signature* based on the instance documents. Then, the signatures associated to the nodes of the two ontologies are compared pairwise, and a similarity score for each pair is generated. This score could then be used to estimate the likelihood of a match between a pair of nodes, under the assumption that the semantics of a node corresponds to the semantics of the instance documents classified under that node. Figure 1 shows the architecture of our system.

The two main issues to be addressed are (1) the representation of signatures and (2) the definition of a suitable comparison metric between signatures. For a long time, the Information Retrieval community has succesfully adopted a "bag of words" approach to effectively represent and compare text documents. We start from there to define a general signature structure and a metric to compare signatures.

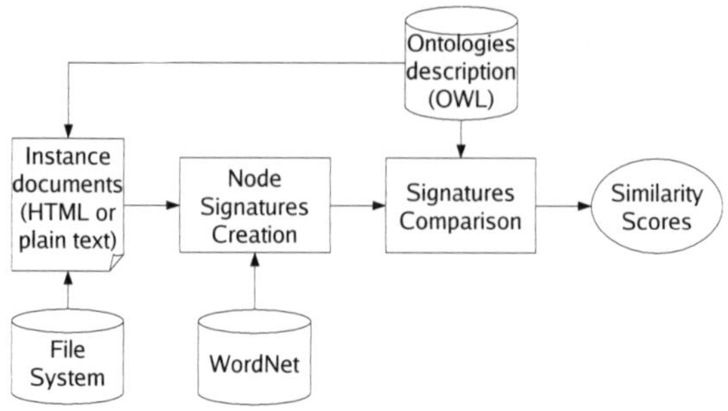

Figure 1: Ontology aligment architecture

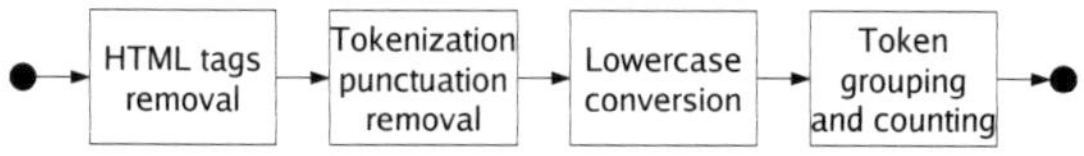

Figure 2: Baseline signature creation

A *signature* is defined as a function $S : K \rightarrow R^+$, mapping a finite set of *keys* (which can be complex objects) to positive real values. With a signature of that form, we can use the *cosine similarity* metric to score the similarity between two signatures:

$$simil(S_1, S_2) = \frac{\sum_p S_1(k_p) S_2(k_p)}{\sqrt{\sum_i S_1(k_i)^2} \cdot \sqrt{\sum_j S_2(k_j)^2}}$$

$$k_p \in K_1 \cap K_2, \; k_i \in K_1, \; k_j \in K_2$$

The cosine similarity formula produces a value in the range [0, 1]. The meaning of that value depends on the algorithm used to build the signature. In particular, there is no predefined threshold that can be used to discriminate matches from non-matches. However, such a threshold could be computed a-posteriori from a statistical analysis of experimental results.

2.1 Signature generation algorithms

For our experiments, we defined and implemented four algorithms to generate signatures. The four algorithms make use of text and language processing techniques of increasing complexity.

2.1.1 Algorithm 1: Baseline signature

The baseline algorithm performs a very simple sequence of text processing, schematically represented in Figure 2.

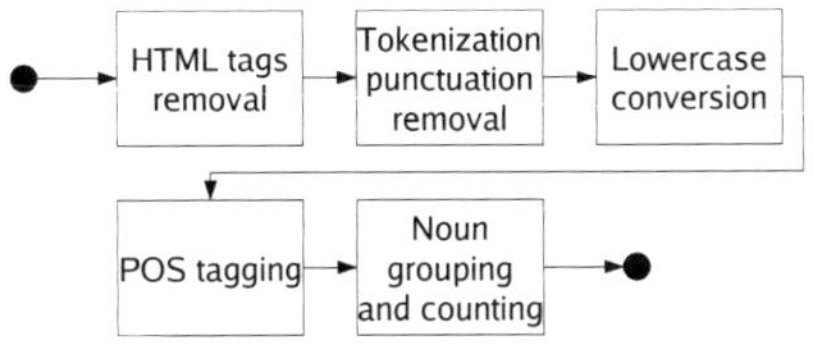

Figure 3: Noun signature creation

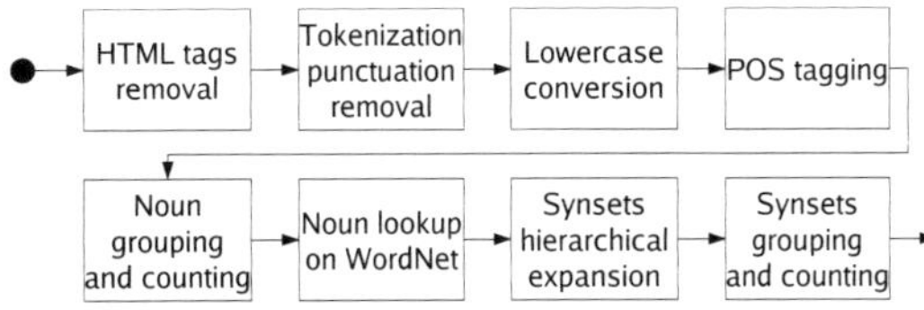

Figure 4: WordNet signature creation

HTML tags are first removed from the instance documents. Then, the texts are tokenized and punctuation is removed. Everything is then converted to lowercase. Finally, the tokens are grouped and counted. The final signature has the form of a mapping table *token* $\rightarrow$ *frequency*.

The main problem we expected with this method is the presence of a lot of noise. In fact, many "irrelevant" words, like determiners, prepositions, and so on, are added to the final signature.

2.1.2 Algorithm 2: Noun signature

To cope with the problem of excessive noise, people in IR often use fixed lists of *stop words* to be removed from the texts. Instead, we introduced a syntax based filter in our chain of processing. The main assuption is that nouns are the words that carry most of the meaning for our kind of document comparison. Thus, we introduced a part-of-speech tagger right after the tokenization module (Figure 3). The results of the tagger are used to discard everything but nouns from the input documents. The part-of-speech tagger we used –QTAG 3.1 (Tufis and Mason, 1998), readily available on the web as a Java library– is a Hidden Markov Model based statistical tagger.

The problems we expected with this approach are related to the high specialization of words in natural language. Different nouns can bear similar meaning, but our system would treat them as if they were completely unrelated words. For example, the words "apple" and "orange" are semantically closer than "apple" and "chair," but a purely syntactic approach would not make any difference between these two pairs. Also, the current method does not include morphological processing, so different inflections of the same word, such as "apple" and "apples," are treated as distinct words.

In further experiments, we also considered verbs, another syntactic category of words bearing a lot of semantics in natural language. We computed signatures with verbs only, and with verbs and nouns together. In both cases, however, the performance of the system was worse. Thus, we will not consider verbs in the rest of the paper.

2.1.3 Algorithm 3: WordNet signature

To address the limitations stated above, we used the WordNet lexical resource (Miller et al., 1990). WordNet is a dictionary where words are linked together by semantic relationships. In WordNet, words are grouped into *synsets*, i.e., sets of synonyms. Each synset can have links to other synsets. These links represent semantic relationships like hypernymy, hyponymy, and so on.

In our approach, after the extraction of nouns and their grouping, each noun is looked up on WordNet (Figure 4). The synsets to which the noun belongs are added to the final signature in place of the noun itself. The signature can also be enriched with the hypernyms of these synsets, up to a specified level. The final signature has the form of a mapping *synset* $\rightarrow$ *value*, where *value* is a weighted sum of all the synsets found.

Two important parameters of this method are related to the hypernym expansion process mentioned above. The first parameter is the maximum level of hypernyms to be added to the signature (*hypernym level*). A hypernym level value of 0 would make the algorithm add only the synsets of a word, without any hypernym, to the signature. A value of 1 would cause the algorithm to add also their parents in the hypernym hierarchy to the signature. With higher values, all the ancestors up to the specified level are added. The second parameter, *hypernym factor*, specifies the damping of the weight of the hypernyms in the expansion process. Our algorithm exponentially dampens the hypernyms, i.e., the weigth of a hypernym decreases exponentially as its level increases. The hypernym factor is the base of the exponential function.

In general, a noun can have more than one sense, e.g., "apple" can be either a fruit or a tree. This is reflected in WordNet by the fact that a noun can belong to multiple synsets. With the current approach, the system cannot decide which

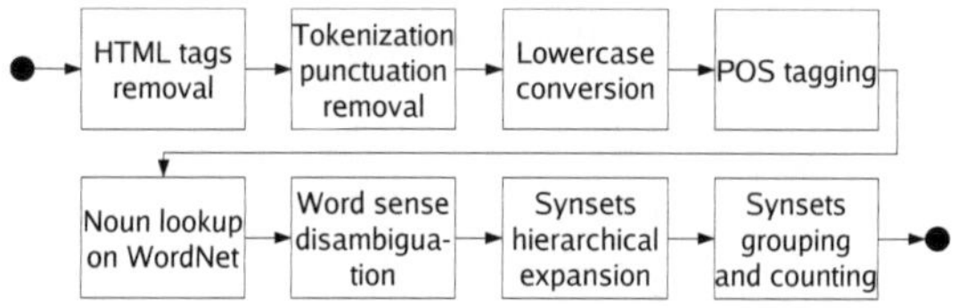

Figure 5: Disambiguated signature creation

sense is the most appropriate, so all the senses of a word are added to the final signature, with a weight inversely proportional to the number of possible senses of that word. This fact potentially introduces *semantic noise* in the signature, because many irrelevant senses might be added to the signature itself.

Another limitation is that a portion of the nouns in the source texts cannot be located in WordNet (see Figure 6). Thus, we also tried a variation (algorithm 3+2) that falls back on to the bare lexical form of a noun if it cannot be found in WordNet. This variation, however, resulted in a slight decrease of performance.

2.1.4 Algorithm 4: Disambiguated signature

The problem of having multiple senses for each word calls for the adoption of word sense disambiguation techniques. Thus, we implemented a word sense disambiguator algorithm, and we inserted it into the signature generation pipeline (Figure 5). For each noun in the input documents, the disambiguator takes into account a specified number of *context words*, i.e., nouns preceding and/or following the target word. The algorithm computes a measure of the *semantic distance* between the possible senses of the target word and the senses of each of its context words, pairwise. A sense for the target word is chosen such that the total distance to its context is minimized. The *semantic distance* between two synsets is defined here as the minimum number of hops in the WordNet hypernym hierarchy connecting the two synsets. This definition allows for a relatively straightforward computation of the semantic distance using WordNet. Other more sophisticated definitions of semantic distance can be found in (Patwardhan et al., 2003). The word sense disambiguation algorithm we implemented is certainly simpler than others proposed in the literature, but we used it to see whether a method that is relatively simple to implement could still help.

The overall parameters for this signature creation algorithm are the same as the WordNet signature algorithm, plus two additional parameters for the word sense disambiguator: *left context length* and *right context length*. They represent respectively how many nouns before and after the target should be taken into account by the disambiguator. If those two parameters are both set to zero, then no context is provided, and the first possible sense is chosen. Notice that even in this case the behaviour of this signature generation algorithm is different from the previous one. In a WordNet signature, every possible sense for a word is inserted, whereas in a WordNet disambiguated signature only one sense is added.

3 Experimental setting

All the algorithms described in the previous section have been fully implemented in a coherent and extensible framework using the Java programming language, and evaluation experiments have been run. This section describes how the experiments have been conducted.

3.1 Test data

The evaluation of ontology matching approaches is usually made difficult by the scarceness of test ontologies readily available in the community. This problem is even worse for instance based approaches, because the test ontologies need also to be "filled" with instance documents. Also, we wanted to test our algorithms with "real world" data, rather than toy examples.

We were able to collect suitable test data starting from the ontologies published by the Ontology Alignment Evaluation Initiative 2005 (Euzenat et al., 2005). A section of their data contained an OWL representation of fragments of the Google, Yahoo, and LookSmart web directories. We "reverse engineered" some of this fragments, in order to reconstruct two consistent trees, one representing part of the Google directory structure, the other representing part of the LookSmart hierarchy. The leaf nodes of these trees were filled with instances downloaded from the web pages classified by the appropriate directories. With this method, we were able to fill 7 nodes of each ontology with 10 documents per node, for a total of 140 documents. Each document came from a distinct web page, so there was no overlap in the data to be compared. A graphical representation of our two test ontologies, *source* and *target*, is shown in Figure 6. The darker outlined nodes are those filled with instance documents. For the sake of readability, the names of the nodes corresponding to real matches are the same. Of course, this information is not used by our algorithms, which adopt a purely instance based approach. Figure 6 also reports the size of the instance documents associated to each node: total number of words, noun tokens, nouns, and nouns covered by WordNet.

3.2 Parameters

The experiments have been run with several combinations of the relevant parameters: number of instance documents per node (5 or 10), algorithm (1 to 4), extracted parts of speech (nouns, verbs, or both), hypernym level (an integer value equal or greater than zero), hypernym factor (a real number), and context length (an integer number equal or greater than zero). Not all of the parameters are applicable to every algorithm. The total number of runs was 90.

4 Results

Each run of the system with our test ontologies produced a set of 49 values, representing the matching score of every pair of nodes containing instances across the two ontologies. Selected examples of these results are shown in Tables 1, 2, 3, and 4. In the experiments shown in those tables, 10 instance documents for each node were used to compute the signatures. Nodes that actually match (identified by the same label, e.g., "Canada" and "Canada") should show high similarity scores, whereas nodes that do not match (e.g., "Canada" and "Dendrochronology"), should have low scores. Better algorithms would have higher scores for matching nodes, and lower score for non-matching ones. Notice that the two nodes "Egypt" and "Pyramid Theories," although intuitively related, have documents that take different perspectives on the subject. So, the algorithms correctly identify the nodes as being different.

Looking at the results in this form makes it difficult to precisely assess the quality of the algorithms. To do so, a statistical analysis has to be performed. For each table of results, let us partition the scores in two distinct sets:

$$A = \{simil(node_i, node_j) \mid \text{real match} = true\}$$

$$B = \{simil(node_i, node_j) \mid \text{real match} = false\}$$

Source node	Target node: Canada	Dendro chronology	Mega liths	Muse ums	Nazca Lines	Pyramid Theories	United Kingdom
Canada	**0.95**	0.89	0.89	0.91	0.87	0.86	0.92
Dendro chronology	0.90	**0.97**	0.91	0.90	0.88	0.87	0.92
Egypt	0.86	0.89	0.91	0.87	0.86	0.88	0.90
Megaliths	0.90	0.91	**0.99**	0.93	0.95	0.94	0.93
Museums	0.89	0.88	0.90	**0.93**	0.88	0.87	0.90
Nazca Lines	0.88	0.88	0.95	0.91	**0.99**	0.93	0.91
United Kingdom	0.87	0.87	0.86	0.88	0.82	0.82	**0.96**

Table 1: Results – Baseline signature algorithm

Source node	Target node: Canada	Dendro chronology	Mega liths	Muse ums	Nazca Lines	Pyramid Theories	United Kingdom
Canada	**0.67**	0.20	0.14	0.35	0.08	0.08	0.41
Dendro chronology	0.22	**0.80**	0.15	0.22	0.09	0.09	0.25
Egypt	0.13	0.23	0.26	0.22	0.17	0.24	0.25
Megaliths	0.28	0.20	**0.85**	0.37	0.22	0.27	0.33
Museums	0.30	0.19	0.18	**0.58**	0.08	0.14	0.27
Nazca Lines	0.13	0.12	0.26	0.18	**0.96**	0.14	0.17
United Kingdom	0.42	0.20	0.17	0.26	0.09	0.11	**0.80**

Table 2: Results – Noun signature algorithm

Source node	Target node: Canada	Dendro chronology	Mega liths	Muse ums	Nazca Lines	Pyramid Theories	United Kingdom
Canada	**0.79**	0.19	0.19	0.38	0.15	0.06	0.56
Dendro chronology	0.26	**0.83**	0.18	0.20	0.16	0.07	0.24
Egypt	0.17	0.24	0.32	0.21	0.31	0.30	0.27
Megaliths	0.39	0.21	**0.81**	0.41	0.40	0.25	0.42
Museums	0.31	0.14	0.17	**0.70**	0.11	0.11	0.26
Nazca Lines	0.24	0.20	0.42	0.29	**0.91**	0.21	0.29
United Kingdom	0.56	0.17	0.22	0.25	0.15	0.08	**0.84**

Table 3: Results – WordNet signature algorithm (hypernym level=0)

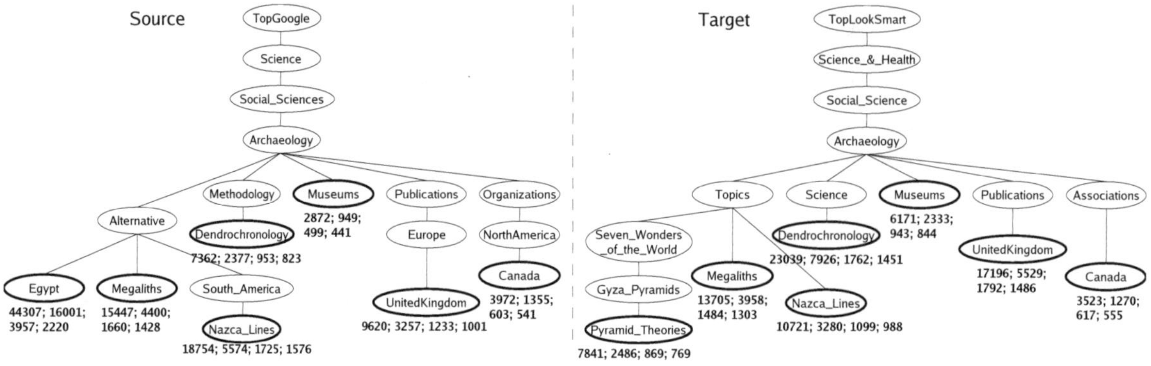

Figure 6: Ontologies used in the experiments. The numbers below the leaves indicate the size of instance documents: # of words; # of noun tokens; # of nouns; # of nouns in WordNet

Source node	Target node: Canada	Dendro chronology	Mega liths	Muse ums	Nazca Lines	Pyramid Theories	United Kingdom
Canada	**0.68**	0.18	0.13	0.33	0.12	0.05	0.44
Dendro chronology	0.23	**0.79**	0.15	0.20	0.14	0.07	0.23
Egypt	0.15	0.23	0.28	0.22	0.27	0.31	0.27
Megaliths	0.30	0.18	**0.84**	0.37	0.34	0.27	0.33
Museums	0.29	0.16	0.15	**0.60**	0.11	0.10	0.24
Nazca Lines	0.20	0.17	0.38	0.26	**0.89**	0.21	0.26
United Kingdom	0.45	0.17	0.18	0.24	0.15	0.08	**0.80**

Table 4: Results – Disambiguated signature algorithm (hypernym level=0, left context=1, right context=1)

With our test data, we would have 6 values in set A and 43 values in set B. Then, let us compute average and standard deviation of the values included in each set. The average of A represents the expected score that the system would assign to a match; likewise, the average of B is the expected score of a non-match. We define the following measure to compare the performance of our matching algorithms, inspired by "effect size" from (VanLehn et al., 2005):

$$\text{discrimination size} = \frac{avg(A) - avg(B)}{stdev(A) + stdev(B)}$$

Higher discrimination values mean that the scores assigned to matches and non-matches are more "far away," making it possible to use those scores to make more reliable decisions about the matching degree of pairs of nodes.

Table 5 shows the values of discrimination size (last column) out of selected results from our experiments. The algorithm used is reported in the first column, and the values of the other relevant parameters are indicated in other columns. We can make the following observations.

- Algorithms 2, 3, and 4 generally outperform the baseline (algorithm 1).
- Algorithm 2 (Noun signature), which still uses a fairly simple and purely syntactical technique, shows a substantial improvement. Algorithm 3 (WordNet signature), which introduces some additional level of semantics, has even better performance.
- In algorithms 3 and 4, hypernym expansion looks detrimental to performance. In fact, the best results are obtained with hypernym level equal to zero (no hypernym expansion).
- The word sense disambiguator implemented in algorithm 4 does not help. Even though disambiguating with some limited context (1 word before and 1 word after) provides slightly better results than choosing the first available sense for a word (context length equal to zero), the overall results are worse than adding all the possible senses to the signature (algorithm 3).
- Using only 5 documents per node significantly degrades the performance of all the algorithms (see the last 5 lines of the table).

5 Conclusions and future work

The results of our experiments point out several research questions and directions for future work,

Alg	Docs	POS	Hyp lev	Hyp fac	L cont	R cont	Avg (A)	Stdev (A)	Avg (B)	Stdev (B)	Discrimination size
1	10						0.96	0.02	0.89	0.03	**1.37**
2	10	noun					0.78	0.13	0.21	0.09	**2.55**
2	10	verb					0.64	0.20	0.31	0.11	1.04
2	10	nn+vb					0.77	0.14	0.21	0.09	2.48
3	10	noun	0				0.81	0.07	0.25	0.12	**3.08**
3	10	noun	1	1			0.85	0.07	0.41	0.12	2.35
3	10	noun	1	2			0.84	0.07	0.34	0.12	2.64
3	10	noun	1	3			0.83	0.07	0.31	0.12	2.80
3	10	noun	2	1			0.90	0.06	0.62	0.11	1.64
3	10	noun	2	2			0.86	0.07	0.45	0.12	2.18
3	10	noun	2	3			0.84	0.07	0.36	0.12	2.56
3	10	noun	3	1			0.95	0.04	0.78	0.08	1.44
3	10	noun	3	2			0.88	0.07	0.52	0.12	1.91
3	10	noun	3	3			0.85	0.07	0.38	0.12	2.45
3+2	10	noun	0	0			0.80	0.09	0.21	0.11	**2.94**
3+2	10	noun	1	2			0.83	0.08	0.30	0.11	2.73
3+2	10	noun	2	2			0.85	0.08	0.39	0.11	2.40
4	10	noun	0		0	0	0.80	0.12	0.24	0.10	2.64
4	10	noun	0		1	1	0.77	0.11	0.22	0.10	**2.67**
4	10	noun	0		2	2	0.77	0.11	0.23	0.10	2.59
4	10	noun	1	2	0	0	0.82	0.10	0.29	0.10	2.56
4	10	noun	1	2	1	1	0.80	0.10	0.34	0.10	2.27
4	10	noun	1	2	2	2	0.80	0.10	0.35	0.10	2.22
1	5	noun					0.93	0.05	0.86	0.04	0.88
2	5	noun					0.66	0.23	0.17	0.08	1.61
3	5	noun	0				0.70	0.17	0.21	0.11	**1.76**
4	5	noun	0		0	0	0.69	0.21	0.20	0.09	1.63
4	5	noun	0		1	1	0.64	0.21	0.18	0.08	1.58

Table 5: Results – Discrimination size

some more specific and some more general. As regards the more specific issues,

- Algorithm 2 does not perform morphological processing, whereas Algorithm 3 does. How much of the improved effectiveness of Algorithm 3 is due to this fact? To answer this question, Algorithm 2 could be enhanced to include a morphological processor.

- The effectiveness of Algorithms 3 and 4 may be hindered by the fact that many words are not yet included in the WordNet database (see Figure 6). Falling back on to Algorithm 2 proved not to be a solution. The impact of the incompleteness of the lexical resource should be investigated and assessed more precisely. Another venue of research may be to exploit different thesauri, such as the ones automatically derived as in (Curran and Moens, 2002).

- The performance of Algorithm 4 might be improved by using more sophisticated word sense disambiguation methods. It would also be interesting to explore the application of the unsupervised method described in (McCarthy et al., 2004).

As regards our long term plans, first, structural properties of the ontologies could potentially be exploited for the computation of node signatures. This kind of enhancement would make our system move from a purely instance based approach to a combined hybrid approach based on schema and instances.

More fundamentally, we need to address the lack of appropriate, domain specific resources that can support the training of algorithms and models appropriate for the task at hand. WordNet is a very general lexicon that does not support domain specific vocabulary, such as that used in geosciences or in medicine or simply that contained in a subontology that users may define according to their interests. Of course, we do not want to develop by hand domain specific resources that we have to change each time a new domain arises.

The crucial research issue is how to exploit extremely scarce resources to build efficient and effective models. The issue of scarce resources makes it impossible to use methods that are succesful at discriminating documents based on the words they contain but that need large corpora for training, for example Latent Semantic Analysis (Landauer et al., 1998). The experiments described in this paper could be seen as providing a *bootstrapped* model (Riloff and Jones, 1999; Ng and Cardie, 2003)—in ML, bootstrapping requires to seed the classifier with a small number of well chosen target examples. We could develop a web spider, based on the work described on this paper, to automatically retrieve larger amounts of training and test data, that in turn could be processed with more sophisticated NLP techniques.

Acknowledgements

This work was partially supported by NSF Awards IIS–0133123, IIS–0326284, IIS–0513553, and ONR Grant N00014–00–1–0640.

References

Eneko Agirre, Olatz Ansa, Eduard Hovy, and David Martinez. 2000. Enriching very large ontologies using the WWW. In *ECAI Workshop on Ontology Learning*, Berlin, August.

Isabel F. Cruz and Afsheen Rajendran. 2003. Exploring a new approach to the alignment of ontologies. In *Workshop on Semantic Web Technologies for Searching and Retrieving Scientific Data, in cooperation with the International Semantic Web Conference.*

Isabel F. Cruz, William Sunna, and Anjli Chaudhry. 2004. Semi-automatic ontology alignment for geospatial data integration. *GIScience*, pages 51–66.

James Curran and Marc Moens. 2002. Improvements in automatic thesaurus extraction. In *Workshop on Unsupervised Lexical Acquisition*, pages 59–67, Philadelphia, PA, USA.

AnHai Doan, Jayant Madhavan, Robin Dhamankar, Pedro Domingos, and Alon Halevy. 2003. Learning to match ontologies on the semantic web. *VLDB Journal*, 12(4):303–319.

Jérôme Euzenat, Heiner Stuckenschmidt, and Mikalai Yatskevich. 2005. Introduction to the ontology alignment evaluation 2005. *http://oaei.inrialpes.fr/2005/results/oaei2005.pdf.*

Eduard Hovy. 2002. Comparing sets of semantic relations in ontology. In R. Green, C. A. Bean, and S. H. Myaeng, editors, *Semantics of Relationships: An Interdisciplinary Perspective*, pages 91–110. Kluwer.

T. C. Hughes and B. C. Ashpole. 2005. The semantics of ontology alignment. *Draft Paper, Lockheed Martin Advanced Technology Laboratories, Cherry Hill, NJ. http://www.atl.lmco.com/projects/ontology/ papers/ SOA.pdf.*

Thomas K. Landauer, Peter W. Foltz, and Darrell Laham. 1998. Introduction to Latent Semantic Analysis. *Discourse Processes*, 25:259–284.

Shuang Liu, Clement Yu, and Weiyi Meng. 2005. Word sense disambiguation in queries. In *ACM Conference on Information and Knowledge Management (CIKM2005)*, Bremen, Germany.

Diana McCarthy, Rob Koeling, Julie Weeds, and John Carroll. 2004. Finding predominant word senses in untagged text. In *42nd Annual Meeting of the Association for Computational Linguistics*, Barcelona, Spain.

G. A. Miller, R. Beckwith, C. Fellbaum, D. Gross, and K. J. Miller. 1990. Introduction to wordnet: an online lexical database. *International Journal of Lexicography*, 3 (4):235–244.

Vincent Ng and Claire Cardie. 2003. Bootstrapping coreference classifiers with multiple machine learning algorithms. In *The 2003 Conference on Empirical Methods in Natural Language Processing (EMNLP-2003).*

Natalya Fridman Noy and Mark A. Musen. 2000. Prompt: Algorithm and tool for automated ontology merging and alignment. In *National Conference on Artificial Intelligence (AAAI).*

Siddharth Patwardhan, Satanjeev Banerjee, and Ted Pedersen. 2003. Using semantic relatedness for word sense disambiguation. In *Fourth International Conference on Intelligent Text Processing and Computational Linguistics (CiCLING-03)*, Mexico City.

Erhard Rahm and Philip A. Bernstein. 2001. A survey of approaches to automatic schema matching. *VLDB Journal*, 10(4):334–350.

Ellen Riloff and Rosie Jones. 1999. Learning dictionaries for information extraction by multi-level bootstrapping. In *AAAI-99, Sixteenth National Conference on Artificial Intelligence.*

Rajen Subba and Sadia Masud. 2004. Automatic generation of a thesaurus using wordnet as a means to map concepts. *Tech report, University of Illinois at Chicago.*

Dan Tufis and Oliver Mason. 1998. Tagging romanian texts: a case study for qtag, a language independent probabilistic tagger. In *First International Conference on Language Resources & Evaluation (LREC)*, pages 589–596, Granada, Spain.

Kurt VanLehn, Collin Lynch, Kay Schulze, Joel Shapiro, Robert Shelby, Linwood Taylor, Donald Treacy, Anders Weinstein, and Mary Wintersgill. 2005. The andes physics tutoring system: Five years of evaluations. In *12th International Conference on Artificial Intelligence in Education*, Amsterdam.

Using the Web as a Phonological Corpus: a case study from Tagalog

Kie Zuraw
Department of Linguistics
UCLA
Los Angeles, U.S.A.
kie@ucla.edu

Abstract

Some languages' orthographic properties allow written data to be used for phonological research. This paper reports on an on-going project that uses a web-derived text corpus to study the phonology of Tagalog, a language for which large corpora are not otherwise available. Novel findings concerning the phenomenon of intervocalic tapping are discussed in detail, and an overview of other phonological phenomena in the language that can be investigated through written data is given.

1 Introduction

Because the field of phonology studies *sound* patterns of languages, corpus-based phonology typically relies on audio corpora. These are expensive to create, and usually must undergo laborious hand-tagging to be useful. For much phonological investigation, there is no way around these harsh facts. Sometimes, however, a language's phonology and orthography conspire to allow phonological data to be gleaned from text. Abigail Cohn and Lisa Lavoie (p.c.), for example, have used text data on English comparatives to determine whether words are treated as monosyllabic, taking suffixal *X-er*, or longer, taking periphrastic *more X*. The cases of interest are words such as *feel* and *fire*, which have a tense or diphthongal nucleus followed by *l* or *r*, and are felt by many English speakers to be longer than monosyllabic. Corpus data on the frequencies of the two comparative types can be used as further evidence on the status of such words.

The Tagalog language (Austronesian, Philippines) exhibits several morphophonological phenomena that are reflected in its spelling. All of these phenomena involve some variation, which makes them ideal for text-corpus study: only with large amounts of data can we investigate the distribution of the variants and search for the factors that condition the variation. See Schachter & Otanes (1972) for basic descriptions of most of these phenomena:

- intervocalic tapping (*d* can become the tap sound [ɾ], spelled *r*, when it is between two vowels): ***d**umi* 'dirt' *ma-**r**umi* 'dirty'
- vowel-height alternations (*o* in final syllables can alternate with *u* in non-final syllables; there is a similar but more complicated *i/e* alternation): *hal**o*** 'mix' *hal**u**-in* 'to be mixed'
- nasal assimilation (a nasal consonant can take on the place of articulation of a following consonant): *pa**m**-butas* 'borer' *pa**n**-damot* 'picker-upper' *pa**ng**-gamas* 'trowel' (*ng* represents the velar nasal [ŋ])
- nasal substitution (stem-initial obstruents can turn into nasals when certain prefixes are added): ***p**ili* 'choosing' *ma-**m**ili* 'to choose'
- syncope (the vowel of a stem's final syllable can be deleted when a suffix is added, and the consonants that consequently become adjacent can undergo changes): *gaw**a*** 'act' *gaw_-in* 'to be done', *ting**i**n* 'look' *tig_n-an* 'to be looked at'
- partial reduplication (when foreign stems that begin with consonant sequences and/or foreign consonants such as *f* un-

dergo copying of the first syllable, the consonant sequence can be simplified and the foreign consonant can be nativized): *nag-**fri**-friendster* ~ *nag-**pi**-friendster* 'using Friendster'

- infix location (in foreign stems beginning with consonant sequences, an infix can go inside or after the consonant sequence): *g-**um**-raduate* ~ *gr-**um**-aduate* 'graduated'
- infix *in* vs. prefix *ni*: *l-**in**-uto* ~ ***ni**-luto* 'to be cooked'
- location of reduplication in prefixed words: ***pa**-pag-lagy-an* ~ *pag-**la**-lagy-an* 'will place' (stem is *lagy*, from *lagay* 'location')

Variation in some of these phenomena has been investigated previously (Ross 1996 for partial reduplication; Rackowski 1999 for location of reduplication), sometimes using dictionary counts to obtain statistics (Zuraw 2002 for vowel height; Zuraw 2000 for nasal substitution). Corpus frequencies of the variants, however, or even basic word frequencies, have not previously been available.

As should be apparent from the examples given above, which are all in normal Tagalog spelling except for the hyphens added to show morpheme boundaries (hyphens are used in Tagalog, but not in the locations shown above), all of these phonological phenomena can be investigated in a text corpus. In most cases, modulo typing errors, we can be confident that the written form represents the writer's intended pronunciation, especially since spell-checking software that would change a writer's original spelling is not widely used for Tagalog, and there is little prescriptive pressure favoring one variant spelling over the other.[1] One area in which we should be cautious is partial reduplication, however: in a spelling such as *nag-fri-friendster*, it is plausible first that the writer might pronounce the stem in a nativized fashion despite preserving the English spelling (e.g., with [p] instead of [f][2]), and second that regardless of intended stem pronunciation, the reduplicant's spelling is merely an echo of the stem's spelling, and does not reflect the writer's pronunciation.

Section 2 below describes how a written corpus of Tagalog was constructed from the web. Section 3 gives results from the corpus on tapping, and Section 4 concludes.

2 Construction of the corpus

Like most of the world's 6,000 or so languages, Tagalog is a language for which carefully constructed, tagged corpora (written or audio) do not exist. However, unlike most of the world's languages, Tagalog has a substantial web presence. As with all web-as-corpus endeavors, there is the drawback that the data will be messier, and there will be more input from non-native speakers than in, say, a newspaper-derived corpus. But in the case of some phenomena, such as infix location, a web corpus is actually preferable to a newspaper-derived corpus (if one existed): the range of loanwords found in formal Tagalog writing is narrower, favoring Spanish loans over English, than that found in the highly informal writing of blogs and web forums. From this informal writing we can obtain data on how the language's grammar is being extended to the novel phonological situations presented by a wide range of English loans.

A previous demonstration project (Ghani, Jones and Mladenić 2004) showed how a corpus of Tagalog can be created from the web by constructing queries designed to target Tagalog-language pages and exclude pages in other languages; the queries are created by using a small seed corpus to estimate word frequencies, and the frequencies are updated as the corpus grows. Kevin Scannell's *An Crúbadán* project (http://borel.slu.edu/crubadan/index.html), which seems to work in a similar fashion, includes a Tagalog language model. BootCaT (Baroni & Bernardini 2004), which is designed to create corpora and discover multi-word terms in specialized domains, such as psychiatry, works similarly, with the added twist that queries use words that are more frequent in the target domain than in a reference corpus. The method used here is similar, though cruder. No attempt is made to exclude pages written partly or even mostly in a language other than Tagalog; many blogs, for instance, are overwhelmingly in English but with occasional sprinklings of Tagalog, and I wanted to obtain these sprinklings, because they are rich in nonce affixed forms of loanwords.[3]

[1] Location of reduplicant is an exception: prescriptively, the reduplicant is adjacent to the root (Tania Azores-Gunter, p.c.).

[2] A Philippine social-networking website similar to friendster.com is jocularly named prendster.com.

[3] I have not conducted any performance comparisons of different language-identification algorithms in pulling Taga-

In order to construct the corpus used here, first a smaller corpus of mainly Tagalog web pages, generously supplied by Rosie Jones (derived from Ghani, Jones and Mladenić 2004) was processed in order to yield estimated word frequencies for Tagalog.

Using these frequencies, a long list of queries composed of frequent words is automatically generated. Each term is at least 12 characters long, including spaces but not including apostrophes or other non-alphabetic characters. A word is chosen from among the most frequent 500 in the starter corpus, with a probability proportional to its log frequency. If this produces a 12-character string, the query is complete. Otherwise, another word is chosen using the same procedure and added to the string, until the threshold of 12 characters is reached. This threshold was selected in order to ensure queries long enough to be specifically Tagalog (e.g., not *sa ng*), but short enough to yield a large number of web hits. Some sample queries: *kami pangulo*, *+at salita oo*,[4] *lalo parang*, *noong akin aklat*. Although these queries are not treated as phrases, the order produced by the query-generator was preserved, because the topmost hits produced by, e.g., *lalo parang* and *parang lalo* are not the same. It is important to "toss the salad"[5] in this way, because the Google search engine that these queries are sent to allows only the top 1,000 results of a query to be viewed.

A program that sends these queries to Google (www.google.com), using the Google web APIs service, was written by Ivan Tam. This returns a maximum of 10,000 URLs (web addresses) per day, because a user's license key allows only 1,000 queries per day, and each query return only 10 results—to see more than the top 10 results for a given query, a new query must be sent, which counts against the day's 1,000. Typically, the number of URLs retrieved was about 5,000. This is because the number of times the program asks to see more results for a given query is determined by the estimated number of results initially reported by Google, but this is often an overestimate. For example, Google may estimate that there are 800 results, and the program will thus ask to see 80 pages of results (using up 80 of the day's queries), but perhaps only 621 results will be obtained. (The program gives the user the option of setting a maximum number of results to obtain per query; setting this number lower makes more efficient use of the day's query quota.)

Tam's program gives the option of taking using Google's option to return, out of any subset of results from one query that are highly similar, just one URL. That option was used here, but no further attempt was made to exclude highly similar results that come from different queries—obviously, this is an area where the procedure could be improved. The program also offers the option, which was used here, to create a separate query to search any crowded hosts (Google tends to show only two results from a single server, returning a "More results from ..." link; in the results returned by the Google Web APIs service, this translates into a non-blank value for `<hostName>`).

The day's URLs are compared against those retrieved so far, and the new ones are extracted. Another part of Tam's program then retrieves the full text of each new URL, although an existing program such as wget could also be used. Because the data of interest in this project are unigram and bigram frequencies, and irrelevant bigrams such as "`a href`" (a frequent bigram in html code) play no role, html stripping was not performed.

The resulting corpus currently has 98,607 pages and an estimated 20 million words of Tagalog (200 million "words" total, but examination of a sample finds that when html tags and non-Tagalog text are removed, about 10% remains). Word frequencies and certain bigram frequencies (e.g., the word+enclitic frequencies discussed below) are obtained from this corpus.

3 Tapping in the corpus

The phenomenon investigated most recently in the corpus is tapping. As mentioned above, Tagalog has a rule taking /d/ to the tap [ɾ] (spelled *r*) between vowels; tap rarely occurs non-intervocalically, except in loanwords (Spanish [ɾ] and [r], and English [ɹ] are usually adapted as [ɾ]). There are no opportunities for *d/r* alternation in affixes, but there are stems that begin or end in *d*, and if a vowel-final prefix or

log-language documents from the web, because this would require hand identification of their results (or of a large body of test documents). Qualitatively, however, the Ghani et al. approach does seem to suffer the same main problem as mine: a sizeable number of documents from Philippine languages other than Tagalog are retrieved.

[4] A "+" was added by hand to a few members of the top-500 list that Google would otherwise ignore because they are common function words in English or another major language. Quotations are placed around words with crucial punctuation, such as apostrophes in contractions.

[5] Thanks to Ivan Tam for this useful metaphor.

vowel-initial suffix is attached, the potential for tapping arises. Tapping has been reported to be variable at the prefix-stem boundary (*ma-**rumi*** 'dirty' vs. *ma-**dahon*** 'leafy') but obligatory at the stem-suffix boundary (*laka**r**-an* 'to be walked on', from *laka**d*** 'walk') (Schachter and Otanes 1972). This is reminiscent of phenomena such as *s*-voicing in Northern Italian, which authors such as Nespor and Vogel (1986) and Peperkamp (1997) have analyzed as involving an asymmetry in how prefixes and suffixes relate to the prosodic word. For the sake of brevity, I will not review the Northern Italian facts here, but will apply an analysis similar to Peperkamp's to the Tagalog tapping case. (Peperkamp points out that prefix/suffix asymmetries always seem to be in this direction: prefixes are prosodically less integrated with stems than are suffixes.)

If we assume, as a first approximation, that a suffix is incorporated into the same prosodic word (p-word) as its stem, while a prefix adjoins to the stem to form a higher p-word, and we further assume that tapping applies only to a vowel-*d*-vowel stretch that is not interrupted by a p-word boundary, then we would predict that tapping occurs at the stem-suffix boundary but not at the prefix-stem boundary:

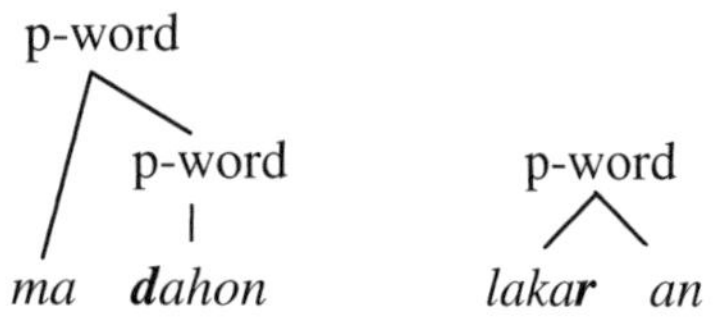

Figure 1. Prosodic structure of prefixed word without tapping vs. suffixed word.

Loosely following Peperkamp, I will assume that this prosodification is derived by a constraint requiring the left edge of any accessed lexical unit (see below) to project the left edge of a p-word. In Optimality Theory terms (Prince & Smolensky 1993/2004), the symmetrical constraint requiring the right edge of an accessed lexical unit to project any prosodic edge is ranked lower (specifically, below an anti-recursion constraint requiring every p-word node to immediately dominate a foot).

3.1 Tapping at the prefix-stem boundary

How can we explain *ma-**rumi***, where tapping does occur at the prefix-stem boundary? In the Northern Italian case, Baroni (2001) found that application of the *s*-voicing rule at the prefix-stem boundary in a reading task was negatively correlated with semantic transparency as determined by a rating task. Baroni's interpretation is that forms with voicing (which tend to be semantically opaque) are treated as morphologically simple. I will follow Baroni loosely in assuming that words like *marumi* are accessed as a single lexical unit (without taking a position on whether that lexical entry contains information about morpheme boundaries). If *marumi* is accessed as a lexical unit—rather than indirectly via *ma-* and *dumi*—then the constraint mentioned above requires only the left edge of the whole word to project a p-word boundary, and the structure is as in Figure 2. Because no p-word boundary interrupts the vowel-*d*-vowel sequence, tapping applies.

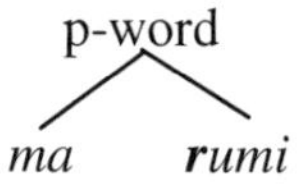

Figure 2. Prosodic structure of prefixed word with tapping.

The corpus does not directly yield judgments of semantic transparency, of course—though indirect measures using the similarity of contexts in which the derived word and its base occur could be examined in future work—but it does yield a statistic that Hay (2003) has argued is closely related to the degree to which a morphologically complex word is treated as a single unit vs. compositionally: the ratio of base frequency to derived-word frequency. Hay argues, based on a series of experiments on English, that when a derived word is more frequent than its morphological base (e.g., English *illegible* vs. *legible*), it is more likely to be accessed through a direct route during processing (direct access to *illegible* rather than access via *in-* and *legible*), and thus more likely to be treated as a single unit phonologically, and more likely to develop independent semantics. The prediction that can be tested in the Tagalog corpus is this: prefixed words that are more frequent than their unprefixed bases are more likely to undergo tapping than prefixed words that are less frequent than their unprefixed bases.

To minimize hand-checking of items, the corpus was searched only for the 592 orthographically distinct prefixed *d*-stem words that appear in a dictionary of Tagalog (English 1986). These words were extracted from the dictionary and put into electronic form by Nikki Foster. The frequency of each word's tapped and untapped form were retrieved from the corpus (e.g., for the dictionary's *i-**d**ipa*, both *idipa* and *iripa*'s frequencies were obtained). Dictionary-listed variants were searched, and certain punctuation was allowed. "Linkers" were also allowed (these are clitics that can become, orthographically, part of the preceding word). The frequency of each word's root, as listed in the dictionary, was also retrieved. (In the case of words with multiple affixes, it is unclear what the immediate morphological predecessor is, so for the sake of simplicity the root, rather than some intermediate form, was used.)

The histograms below show how many prefixed words display each range of tapping rates in the corpus, from 0 (always *d*) to 1 (always *r*). They demonstrate the predicted influence of derived/base frequency ratio on tapping rate: when the prefixed word is more frequent than its root (Figure 3), a high rate of tapping predominates (strongly), whereas when the root is more frequent than the prefixed word (Figure 4), a low rate of tapping predominates (weakly):

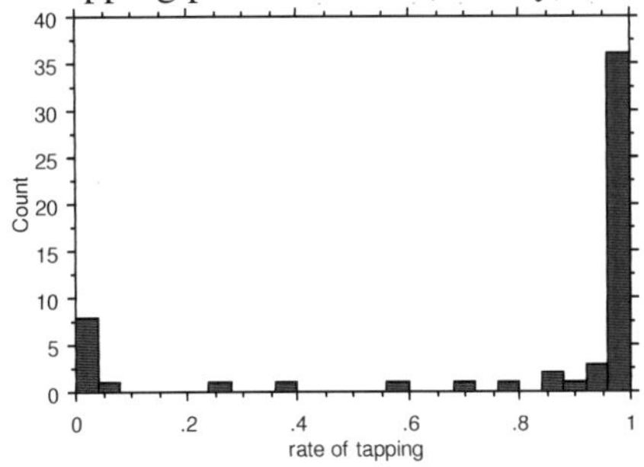

Figure 3. Distribution of tapping rate in prefixed words that are *more* frequent than their bases.

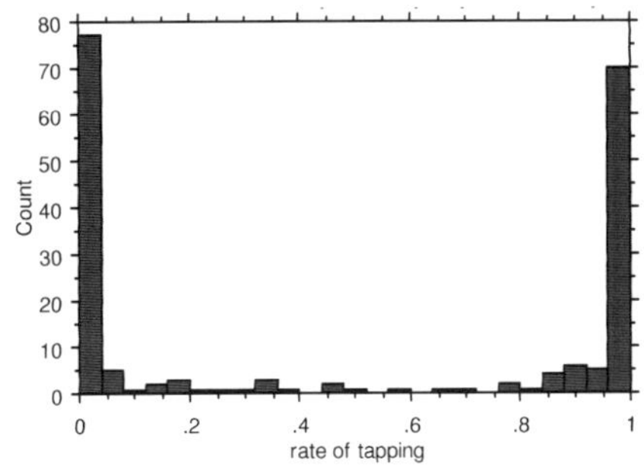

Figure 4. Distribution of tapping rate in prefixed words that are *less* frequent than their bases.

Interestingly, in both cases the rates of tapping cluster near 0 and 1—intermediate rates are relatively rare. The data above are limited to words with a corpus frequency of at least 10, so that each word had a fair chance of displaying an intermediate rate of tapping if that were its true behavior. This suggests that the great majority of prefixed words in Tagalog are lexicalized as either undergoing or not undergoing tapping (or, depending on what form lexical entries in fact take, as having one prosodic structure or the other). This is rather different from the Northern Italian situation discovered by Baroni, where many words robustly vary, even within a single speaker.

Words with a corpus frequency of less than 10, which are almost all less frequent than their bases, show a preference of non-tapping, as expected:

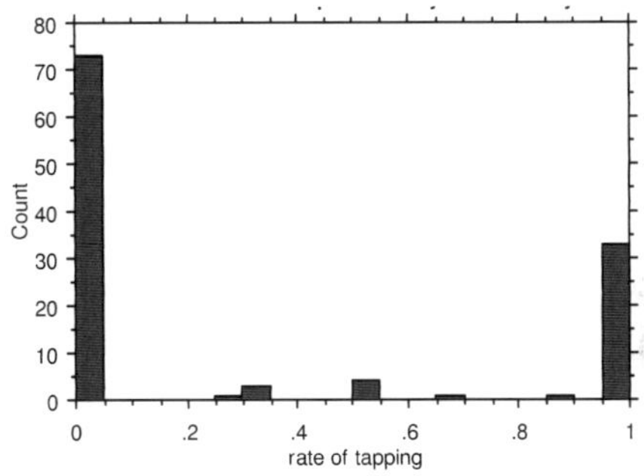

Figure 5. Distribution of tapping rate in prefixed words with corpus frequency < 10 (nearly all are less frequent than their bases).

Hay argues that it is relative frequency of a derived word and its base, not raw frequency of the derived word, that models of lexical access predict to have an effect on word decomposability. In the present case, raw frequency does also have a strong effect on whether a prefixed word belongs to the tapping or non-tapping categories, but raw and relative frequency are themselves highly correlated. In order to verify that relative frequency has an effect independent of raw frequency, the prefixed words were divided into 28 categories according to the log of their raw frequency (0 to <0.1, 0.3 to <0.4, 0.4 to <0.5, etc.). Within each category, the percentage of words *less* frequent than their bases that undergo tapping >95% of the time and the percentage of words *more* frequent than their bases that undergo tapping >95% of the time were calculated. The prediction is that the second percentage should be higher—that is, words matched for raw frequency should be more likely to undergo tapping if they are more frequent than their bases—and this was borne out in a Wilcoxon signed-rank test ($p<.05$). The contribution of raw frequency remains to be further explored.

3.2 Tapping at the stem-suffix boundary

Tapping was examined in a similar fashion at the stem-suffix boundary. From English's (1986) dictionary, 160 native-etymology roots that end in *d* were extracted, and the corpus was searched for any suffixed forms of these roots (with or without additional prefixes and infixes). As expected from Schachter and Otanes's (1972) description, tapping is indeed nearly obligatory at the stem-suffix boundary, as shown in Figure 6 (which again shows only words with corpus frequency of at least 10):

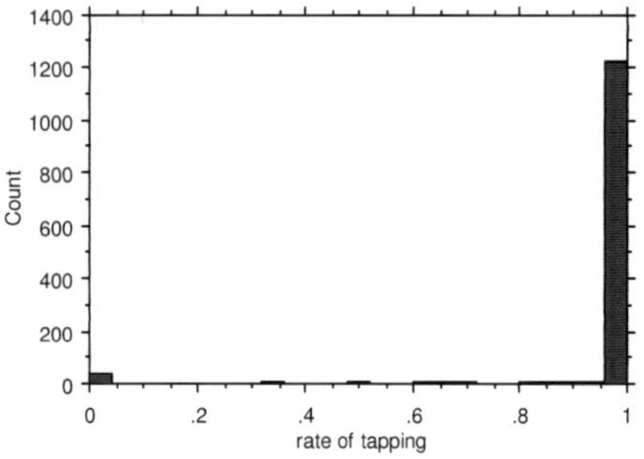

Figure 6. Distribution of tapping rate in suffixed words.

Because of the relative ease of searching for suffixed forms (there are only two productive native suffixes in Tagalog, *-in* and *-an*, so a simple regular expression can find all the suffixed forms of any root), the counts here are much higher than in the prefix-stem case—compare the scales of the vertical axes in the histograms—and we can look more closely at the 124 words—a minority so small it is largely invisible in Figure 6—that do not uniformly undergo tapping at the stem-suffix boundary. Rate of tapping among these 124 words turns out to be weakly but significantly correlated with the log ratio of suffix-word frequency to root frequency (Spearman's rho=.534, $p<.001$), as predicted by Hay's view of phonological integration.

There are multiple possible interpretations for this result under the prosodic account given above. Perhaps stem and suffix do always form a single p-word, but paradigm-uniformity effects (e.g., Steriade 2000) can, if sufficiently strong, block tapping even within a p-word. Or, perhaps the requirement that a suffix be integrated into the prosodic word can itself be overridden, occasionally, by frequency effects demanding a compositional treatment of an affixed word that is less frequent than its base.[6] It is also possible that all the "nontapping" here represents typographical errors, but that there is a frequency effect on errors such that the more frequent a base relative to the word it is nested inside, the more likely that the base's spelling is preserved.

3.3 Tapping at the stem-stem boundary

The prosodic system assumed above (with some constraints not mentioned there), allows a combination of two stems to have either of the prosodic structures shown in Figure 7, with the choice depending on whether the combination is accessed as a single lexical unit. But in either case, a p-word boundary separates the two stems, and thus tapping is not expected on either side of the stem-stem boundary.

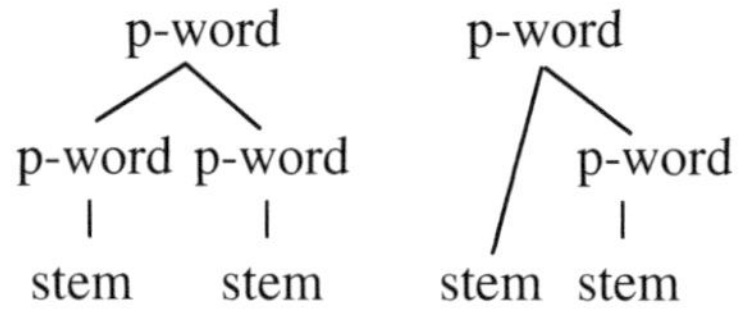

Figure 7. Two possible prosodic structures for compound or two-syllable reduplication.

There are two places where a stem+stem combination could arise in Tagalog. One is in compounds, such as *basag-ulo* 'fight' (lit. *breaking-head*), where each member bears a separate stress. If we assume, following most previous work on the p-word, that dominating a stressed syllable is a necessary feature of a p-word (though not sufficient, since a single p-word may contain multiple stresses), this is consistent with a p-word+p-word prosodic structure. Lacking a list of compounds, however, I found it impractical to search for compounds in the corpus (though this is a project for the future).

The second place where stem-stem boundaries arguably arise is in two-syllable reduplication, which occurs in a variety of morphological constructions, including reduplication by itself: e.g. *pa-balik-balik* 'recurrent', from *balik* 'return'. In these reduplications, each copy bears a stress. We would therefore expect that tapping should not occur at the boundary between the two redu-

[6] In Hay's view, relative frequency is not epiphenomenal, but rather determines the mode of lexical access (direct or indirect route) and thus a word's behavior. It is also possible, of course, that relative frequency is only the symptom of some underlying property of words, or that there is feedback between frequency and the properties that influence it.

plicants. This is indeed what is found, as shown in the histogram below, though the data come mostly from stem-initial *d* cases (e.g., *dagli-**d**agli* 'right away'); there were only 5 stem-final *d* cases that met the frequency threshold (e.g., *aga**d**-agad* 'immediately'):[7]

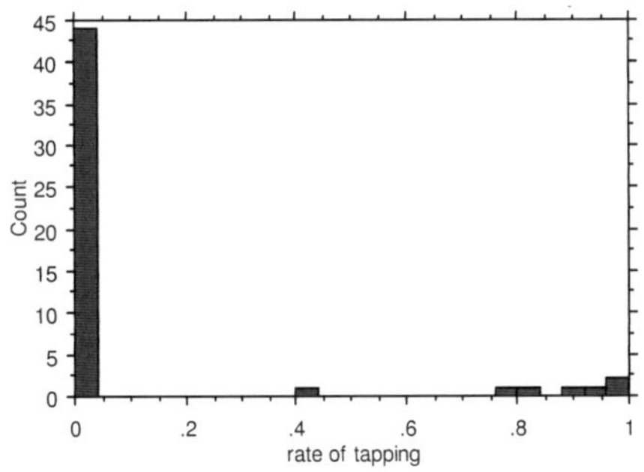

Figure 8. Distribution of tapping rate at reduplicant-reduplicant boundary (two-syllable reduplication).

The lack of tapping is unlikely to be a reduplicative identity effect (Wilbur 1973, McCarthy and Prince 1995), because tapping is blocked even when the other copy of the same consonant does undergo tapping because of an adjacent prefix or suffix (*ka-aga**d**-aga**r**-an, ka-**r**aga-**d**aga-_n* [glosses unknown—English's dictionary contains both roots but not these derivatives of them]).

The lack of tapping is also probably not due to the reduplicated forms' low frequency: most are indeed less frequent than their bases, but it was seen above that prefixed words that are less frequent than their bases undergo tapping almost as often as not.

3.4 Tapping in clitics

There are two enclitics in Tagalog that begin with /d/: *din* 'also' and *daw* '(reported speech)'. Each has a tap-initial allomorph (*rin*, *raw*). There is reported to be variation between the two allomorphs even after consonant-final words (Schachter and Otanes 1972). So far, I have examined in the corpus only *din/rin* after vowel-final words.

All bigrams whose second word is *din* or *rin* were extracted from the corpus. Variation was indeed found, but unlike in the prefix+stem case, where the variation was highly polarized—with most words having one strongly dominant behavior—in the word+clitic case the variation is continuous (again, only bigrams with a corpus frequency of at least 10 are shown):

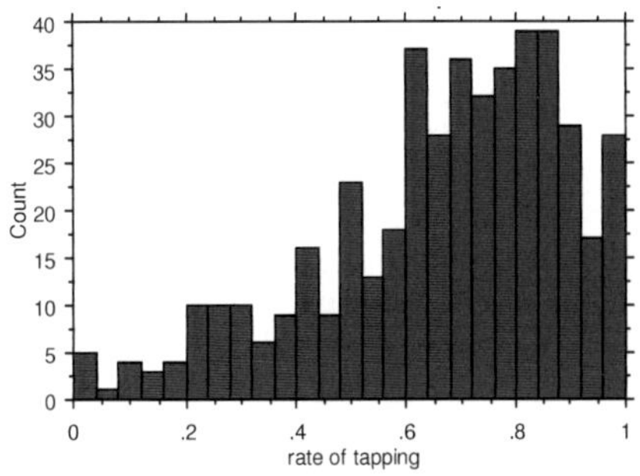

Figure 9. Distribution of tapping rate at word-clitic boundary.

One interpretation is that most word+clitic combinations are not lexicalized, and their tapping behavior is determined on the fly. The correlation between the log ratio of bigram to base word frequency and the rate of tapping, though very weak, is significant (Spearman's rho=.197, $p<.0001$). If we look at enclitic+din/rin combinations (where the first enclitic ends in a vowel, as in ... *pa rin* '... still also'), which display similarly gradient variation, the correlation is stronger, though p is larger because there are fewer data points (Spearman's rho=.527, $p<.05$).

4 Conclusion

This paper has presented one case study, on Tagalog tapping, of phonological research using a written, web-derived corpus. Several aspects of the investigation depended crucially on the web-as-corpus method. Because of economic constraints, the only realistic way to assemble a large corpus of a language like Tagalog is currently by taking text from the web. And only a large corpus makes it possible to ask questions such as "how does the frequency ratio of a derived word to its base affect the application of a phonological rule?" The two different patterns of variation—polarized in the stem+prefix case, continuous in the word+enclitic case—would have been very difficult to discover without corpus data.

This Tagalog corpus has already been used to investigate infixation in loans that begin with consonant clusters (Zuraw 2005). There, as mentioned in Section 2, the web-based nature of the

[7] The interpretation of stem-final *d* cases is complicated by the fact that p-words spelled with an initial vowel are usually actually glottal-stop initial. Thus, *aga**d**-agad* can be pronounced with a glottal stop (*agad-[ʔ]agad*), so that the medial *d* is not truly intervocalic.

corpus was of more than practical importance, because a large quantity of highly informal writing—unlikely to be found in a traditionally constructed written corpus—was needed.

The corpus is also being used in ongoing work on nasal substitution, and will be used in the future to investigate the other phenomena listed in Section 1. The corpus will also continue to grow; there seems to be little danger of running out of Tagalog-language web space to search in the foreseeable future.

Acknowledgement

Thanks to research assistant Ivan Tam for programming that made this project possible, and to research assistant Nikki Foster for data entry. For valuable discussion about tapping, thanks to Colin Wilson, Bruce Hayes, and participants the UCLA phonology seminar. Thanks also to two anonymous reviewers for several ideas that have been incorporated into the paper.

References

Baroni, Marco (2001). The representation of prefixed forms in the Italian lexicon: Evidence from the distribution of intervocalic [s] and [z] in northern Italian. In Geert Booij and Jaap van Marle (eds.), *Yearbook of Morphology* 1999, Springer, Dordrecht: 121-152.

Baroni, Marco and S. Bernardini (2004). BootCaT: Bootstrapping corpora and terms from the web. *Proceedings of LREC 2004.*

English, Leo (1986). *Tagalog-English Dictionary.* Congregation of the Most Holy Redeemer, Manila. Distributed by (Philippine) National Book Store.

Ghani, Rayid, Rosie Jones & Dunja Mladenić (2004). Building minority language corpora by learning to generate Web search queries. *Knowledge and Information Systems* 7: 56-83.

Hay, Jennifer (2003). *Causes and Consequences of Word Structure.* Routledge, New York and London.

McCarthy, John & Alan Prince (1995). Faithfulness and reduplicative identity. *Papers in Optimality Theory, UMass Occasional Papers in Linguistics* 18: 249-348

Nespor, Marina and Irene Vogel (1986). *Prosodic Phonology.* Foris, Dordrecht.

Peperkamp, Sharon (1997). *Prosodic Words.* Holland Academic Graphics, The Hague.

Prince, Alan and Paul Smolensky (1993/2004). *Optimality Theory: Constraint Interaction in Generative Grammar.* Blackwell.

Rackowski, Andrea (1999). Morphological optionality in Tagalog aspectual reduplication. *Papers on Morphology and Syntax, Cycle Two, MIT Working Papers in Linguistics* 34: 107-136.

Ross, Kie (1996). Floating phonotactics: infixation and reduplication in Tagalog loanwords. UCLA M.A. thesis.

Schachter, Paul and Fe Otanes (1972) *Tagalog Reference Grammar.* University of California Press, Berkeley.

Steriade, Donca (2000). Paradigm Uniformity and the phonetics/phonology boundary. In Janet Pierrehumbert and Michael Broe (eds.), *Papers in Laboratory Phonology* vol. 6, Cambridge University Press, Cambridge.

Wilbur, Ronnie Bring (1973). *The Phonology of Reduplication.* Indiana University Linguistics Club, Bloomington.

Zuraw, Kie (2000). Patterned exceptions in phonology. UCLA Ph.D. dissertation.

Zuraw, Kie (2002). Aggressive reduplication. *Phonology* 19: 395-439.

Zuraw, Kie (2005). The role of phonetic knowledge in phonological patterning: Corpus and survey evidence from Tagalog. Manuscript, UCLA.

Web Corpus Mining by instance of Wikipedia

Rüdiger Gleim, Alexander Mehler & Matthias Dehmer
Bielefeld University, D-33615 Bielefeld, Germany
Ruediger.Gleim@uni-bielefeld.de
Alexander.Mehler@uni-bielefeld.de
Technische Universität Darmstadt, Fachbereich Informatik
dehmer@tk.informatik.tu-darmstadt.de

Abstract

In this paper we present an approach to structure learning in the area of web documents. This is done in order to approach the goal of webgenre tagging in the area of web corpus linguistics. A central outcome of the paper is that purely structure oriented approaches to web document classification provide an information gain which may be utilized in combined approaches of web content and structure analysis.

1 Introduction

In order to reliably judge the collocative affinity of linguistic items, it has to be considered that judgements of this kind depend on the scope of certain genres or registers. According to Stubbs (2001), words may have different collocates in different *text types* or *genres* and therefore may signal one of those genres when being observed. Consequently, corpus analysis requires, amongst others, a comparison of occurrences in a given text with typical occurrences in other texts of the same genre (Stubbs, 2001, p. 120).

This raises the question how to judge the membership of texts, in which occurrences of linguistic items are observed, to the genres involved. Evidently, because of the size of the corpora involved, this question is only adequately answered by reference to the area of *automatic* classification. This holds all the more for web corpus linguistics (Kilgarriff and Grefenstette, 2003; Baroni and Bernardini, 2006) where large corpora of web pages, whose membership in *webgenres* is presently unknown, have to be analyzed. Consequently, web corpus linguistics faces two related task:

1. *Exploration:* The task of initially *exploring* which webgenres actually exist.

2. *Categorization:* The task of *categorizing* hypertextual units according to their membership in the genres being explored in the latter step.

In summary, web corpus linguistics is in need of webgenre-sensitive corpora, that is, of corpora in which for the textual units being incorporated the membership to webgenres is annotated. This in turn presupposes that these webgenres are first of all explored.

Currently to major classes of approaches can be distinguished: On the one hand, we find approaches to the categorization of *macro structures* (Amitay et al., 2003) such as web hierarchies, directories and corporate sites. On the other hand, this concerns the categorization of *micro structures* as, for example, single web pages (Kleinberg, 1999) or even page segments (Mizuuchi and Tajima, 1999). The basic idea of all these approaches is to perform categorization as a kind of function learning for mapping web units *above*, *on* or *below* the level of single pages onto at most one predefined category (e.g. genre label) per unit (Chakrabarti et al., 1998). Thus, these approaches focus on the categorization task while disregarding the exploration task. More specifically, the majority of these approaches utilizes *text categorization* methods in conjunction with HTML markup, metatags and link structure beyond bag-of-word representations of the pages' wording as input of feature selection (Yang et al., 2002) – in some cases also of linked pages (Fürnkranz, 1999).

What these approaches are missing is a more general account of web document structure as a source of genre-oriented categorization. That is, they solely map web units onto feature vectors by disregarding their structure. This includes linkage beyond pairwise linking as well as document internal structures according to the Document Object Model (DOM). A central pitfall of this approach is that it disregards the impact of genre membership to document structure and, thus, the signalling of the former by the latter (Ventola, 1987). Therefore a structure-sensitive approach is needed in the area of corpus linguistics which allows for automatic webgenre tagging. That is, an approach which takes both levels of structuring of web documents into account: On the level of their hyperlink-based linkage *and* on the level of their internal structure.

In this paper we present an algorithm as a preliminary step for tackling the exploration and categorization task together. More specifically, we present an approach to unsupervised structure learning which uses tree alignment algorithms as similarity kernels and cluster analysis for class detection. The paper includes a comparative study of several approaches to tree alignment as a source of similarity measuring of web documents. Its central topics are:

- *To what extent is it possible to predict the membership of a web document in a certain genre (or register) solely on grounds of its structure when its lexical content and other content bearing units are completely deleted?* In other words, we ask to what extent structure signals membership in genre.

- A more methodical question regards the choice of appropriate measures of structural similarity to be included into structure learning. In this context, we comparatively study several variants of measuring similarities of trees, that is, *tree edit distance* as well as a class of algorithms which are based on tree linearizations as input to *sequence alignment*.

Our overall findings hint at two critical points: First, there is a significant contribution of structure-oriented methods to webgenre categorization which is unexplored in predominant approaches. Second, and most surprisingly, all methods analyzed toughly compete with a method based on random linearization of input documents.

Why is this research important for web corpus linguistics? An answer to this question can be outlined as follows:

- We explore a further resource of reliably tagging web genres and registers, respectively, in the form of document structure.

- We further develop the notion of *webgenre* and thus help to make document structure accessible to collocation and other corpus linguistic analyses.

In order to support this argumentation, we first present a structure insensitive approach to web categorization in section (2). It shows that this insensitivity systematically leads to multiple categorizations which cannot be traced back to ambiguity of category assignment. In order to solve this problem, an alternative approach to structure learning is presented in sections (3.1), (3.2) and (3.3). This approach is evaluated in section (3.4) on grounds of a corpus of Wikipedia articles. The reason for utilizing this test corpus is that the content-based categories which the explored web documents belong to are known so that we can apply the classical apparatus of evaluation of web mining. The final section concludes and prospects future work.

2 Hypertext Categorization

The basic assumption behind present day approaches to hypertext categorization is as follows: Web units of similar function/content tend to have similar structures. The central problem is that these structures are not directly accessible by segmenting and categorizing *single web pages*. This is due to *polymorphism* and its reversal relation of *discontinuous manifestation*: Generally speaking, polymorphism occurs if the same (hyper-)textual unit manifests several categories. This one-to-many relation of expression and content units is accompanied by a reversal relation according to which the same content or function unit is distributed over several expression units. This combines to a many-to-many relation between explicit, manifesting web structure and implicit, manifested functional or content-based structure.

Our hypothesis is that if polymorphism is a prevalent characteristic of web units, web pages cannot serve as input of categorization since polymorphic pages simultaneously instantiate several categories. Moreover, these multiple categorizations are not simply resolved by segmenting the focal pages, since they possibly manifest categories only discontinuously so that their features do not provide a sufficient discriminatory power. In other words: We expect polymorphism and discontinuous manifestation to be accompanied by many multiple categorizations without being reducible to the problem of disambiguating category assignments. In order to show this, we perform a categorization experiment according to the classical setting of function learning, using a corpus of the genre of *conference websites*. Since these websites serve recurrent functions (e.g. *paper submission*, *registration* etc.) they are expected to be structured homogeneously on the basis of stable, recurrent patterns. Thus, they can be seen as good candidates of categorization.

The experiment is performed as follows: We apply support vector machine (SVM) classification which proves to be successful in case of sparse, high dimensional and noisy feature vectors (Joachims, 2002). SVM classification is performed with the help of the LibSVM (Hsu et al., 2003). We use a corpus of 1,078 English conference websites and 28,801 web pages. Hypertext representation is done by means of a bag-of-features approach using about 85,000 lexical and 200 HTML features. This representation was done with the help of the HyGraph system which explores websites and maps them onto hypertext graphs (Mehler and Gleim, 2005). Following (Hsu et al., 2003), we use a R*adial* B*asis* F*unction* kernel and make optimal parameter selection based on a minimization of a 5-fold cross validation error. Further, we perform a binary categorization for each of the 16 categories based on 16 training sets of pos./neg. examples (see table 1). The size of the training set is 1,858 pages (284 sites); the size of the test set is 200 (82 sites). We perform 3 experiments:

1. *Experiment A – one against all:* First we apply a one against all strategy, that is, we use $X \setminus Y_i$ as the set of negative examples for learning category C_i where X is the set of all training examples and Y_i is the set of positive examples of C_i. The results are listed in table (1). It shows the expected low level of effectivity: recall and precession perform very low on average. In three cases the classifiers fail completely. This result is confirmed when looking at column A of table (2): It shows the number of pages with up to 7 category assignments. In the majority of cases no category could be applied at all – only one-third of the pages was categorized.

Category	rec.	prec.
Abstract(s)	0.2	1.0
Accepted Papers	0.3	1.0
Call for Papers	0.1	1.0
Committees	0.5	0.8
Contact Information	0	0
Exhibition	0.4	1.0
Important Dates	0.8	1.0
Invited Talks	0	0
Menu	0.7	0.7
Photo Gallery	0	0
Program, Schedule	0.8	1.0
Registration	0.9	1.0
Sections, Sessions, Plenary etc.	0.1	0.3
Sponsors and Partners	0	0
Submission Guidelines etc.	0.5	0.8
Venue, Travel, Accommodation	0.9	1.0

Table 1: The categories of the *conference website genre* applied in the experiment.

2. *Experiment B – lowering the discriminatory power:* In order to augment the number of categorizations, we lowered the categories' selectivity by restricting the number of negative examples per category to the number of the corresponding positive examples by sampling the negative examples according to the sizes of the training sets of the remaining categories. The results are shown in table (2): The number of zero categorizations is dramatically reduced, but at the same time the number of pages mapped onto more than one category increases dramatically. There are even more than 1,000 pages which are mapped onto more than 5 categories.

3. *Experiment C – segment level categorization:* Thirdly, we apply the classifiers trained on the monomorphic training pages on segments derived as follows: Pages are segmented into spans of at least 30 tokens reflecting segment borders according to the third level of the pages' document object model trees. Column C of table (2) shows that this scenario does not solve the problem of multiple categorizations since it falls back to the problem of zero categorizations. Thus, polymorphism is not resolved by simply segmenting pages, as other segmentations along the same line of constraints confirmed.

There are competing interpretations of these results: The category set may be judged to be wrong. But it reflects the most differentiated set applied so far in this area. Next, the representation model

number of categorizations	A page level	B page level	C segment level
0	12,403	346	27,148
1	6,368	2387	9,354
2	160	5076	137
3	6	5258	1
4	0	3417	0
5	0	923	0
6	0	1346	0
7	0	184	0

Table 2: The number of pages mapped onto $0, 1, ..., 7$ categories in experiment A, B and C.

may be judged to be wrong, but actually it is usually applied in text categorization. Third, the categorization method may be seen to be ineffective, but SVMs are known to be one of the most effective methods in this area. Further, the classifiers may be judged to be wrong – of course the training set could be enlarged, but already includes about 2,000 manually selected monomorphic training units. Finally, the focal units (i.e. web pages) may be judged to be unsystematically polymorph in the sense of manifesting several logical units. It is this interpretation which we believe to be supported by the experiment.

If this interpretation is true, the structure of web documents comes into focus. This raises the question, what can be gained at all when exploring the visible structuring of documents as found on the web. That is, what is the information gain when categorizing documents solely based on their structures. In order to approach this question we perform an experiment in structure-oriented classification in the next section. As we need to control the negative impact of polymorphism, we concentrate on monomorphic pages which uniquely belong to single categories. This can be guaranteed with the help of Wikipedia articles which, with the exception of special disambiguation pages, only address one topic respectively.

3 Structure-Based Categorization

3.1 Motivation

In this section we investigate how far a corpus of documents can be categorized by solely considering the explicit document structure without any textual content. It is obvious that we cannot expect the results to reach the performance of content based approaches. But if this approach allows to significantly distinguish between categories in contrast to a reference random decider we can conclude that the involvement of structure information may positively affect categorization performance. A positive evaluation can be seen to motivate an implementation of the *Logical Document Structure (LDS) algorithm* proposed by Mehler et al. (2005) who include graph similarity measuring as its kernel. We expect the same experiment to perform significantly better on the LDS instead of the explicit structures. However this experiment can only be seen as a first attempt. Further studies with larger corpora are required.

3.2 Experiment setup

In our experiment, we chose a corpus of articles from the German Wikipedia addressing the following categories:

- *American Presidents* (41 pages)
- *European Countries* (50 pages)
- *German Cities* (78 pages)
- *German Universities* (93 pages)

With the exception of the first category most articles, being represented as a HTML web page, share a typical, though not deterministic visible structure. For example a Wikipedia article about a city contains an info box to the upper right which lists some general information like district, population and geographic location. Furthermore an article about a city contains three or more sections which address the history, politics, economics and possibly famous buildings or persons. Likewise there exist certain design *guidelines* by the Wikipedia project to write articles about countries and universities. However these guidelines are not always followed or they are adapted from one case to another. Therefore, a categorization cannot rely on definite markers in the content. Nevertheless, the expectation is that a human reader, once he has seen a few samples of each category, can with high probability guess the category of an article by simple looking at the layout or visible structure and ignoring the written content. Since the layout (esp. the structure) of a web page is encoded in HTML we consider the structure of their DOM[1]-trees for our categorization experiment. If two articles of the same category share a common visible structure, this should lead to a significant similarity of

[1] *Document Object Model.*

the DOM-trees. The articles of category 'American Presidents' form an exception to this principle up to now because they do not have a typical structure. The articles about the first presidents are relatively short whereas the articles about the recent presidents are much more structured and complex. We include this category to test how well a structure based categorizer performs on such diverse structurations. We examine two corpus variants:

I. All HTML-Tags of a DOM-tree are used for similarity measurement.

II. Only those HTML-tags of a DOM-tree are used which have an impact on the visible structure (i.e. inline tags like *font* or *i* are ignored).

Both cases, I and II, do not include any text nodes. That is, all lexical content is ignored. By distinguishing these two variants we can examine what impact these different degrees of expressiveness have on the categorization performance.

3.3 Distance measurement and clustering

The next step of the experiment is marked by a pairwise similarity measurement of the wikipedia articles which are represented by their DOM-trees according to the two variants described in section 3.2. This allows to create a distance matrix which represents the (symmetric) distances of a given article to any other. In a subsequent and final step the distance matrix will be clustered and the results analyzed.

How to measure the similarity of two DOM-trees? This raises the question what *exactly* the subject of the measurement is and how it can be adequately modeled. Since the DOM is a tree and the order of the HTML-tags matters, we choose ordered trees. Furthermore we want to represent what tag a node represents. This leads to ordered labeled trees for representation. Since trees are a common structure in various areas such as image analysis, compiler optimization and bio informatics (i.e. RNA analysis) there is a high interest in methods to measure the similarity between trees (Tai, 1979; Zhang and Shasha, 1989; Klein, 1998; Chen, 2001; Höchsmann et al., 2003). One of the first approaches with a reasonable computational complexity was introduced by Tai (1979) who extended the problem of sequence edit distance to trees.

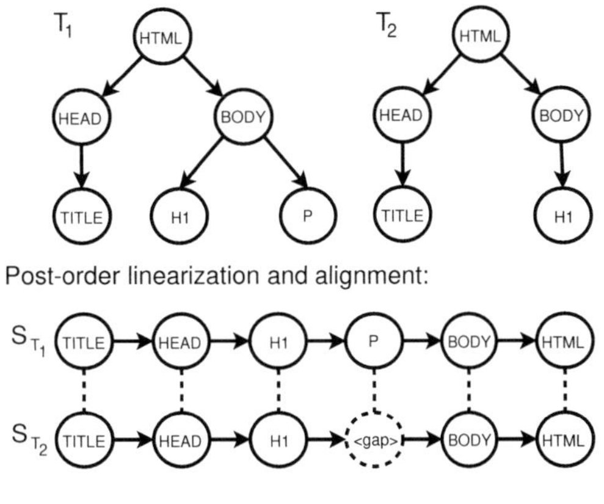

Figure 1: An example for Post-order linearization and sequence alignment.

The following description of tree edit distances is due to Bille (2003): The principle to compute the edit distance between two trees T_1, T_2 is to successively perform elementary edit operations on the former tree to turn it into the formation of the latter. The edit operations on a given tree T are as follows: *Relabel* changes the label of a node $v \in T$. *Delete* deletes a non-root node $v \in T$ with a parent node $w \in T$. Since v is being deleted, its child nodes (if any) are inserted as children of node w. Finally the *Insert* operation marks the complement of delete. Next, an *edit script* S is a list of consecutive edit operations which turn T_1 into T_2. Given a cost function for each edit operation the cost of S is the sum of its elementary operation costs. The *optimal edit script* (there is possibly more than one) between T_1 and T_2 is given by the edit script of minimum cost which equals the *tree edit distance*.

There are various algorithms known to compute the edit distance (Tai, 1979; Zhang and Shasha, 1989; Klein, 1998; Chen, 2001). They vary in computational complexity and whether they can be used for general purpose or under special restrictions only (which allows for better optimization). In this experiment we use the general-purpose algorithm of Zhang and Shasha (1989) which shows a complexity of $O(|T_1||T_2|min(L_1, D_1)min(L_2, D_2))$ where $|T_i|$, L_i, D_i denote the number of nodes, the number of leafs and the depth of the trees respectively.

The approach of tree edit distance forms a good balance between accurate distance measurement of trees and computational complexity. However, especially for large corpora it might be useful to examine how well other (i.e. faster) methods perform. We therefore consider another class of algorithms for distance measurement which are based on sequence alignments via dynamic programming. Since this approach is restricted to the comparison of sequences, a suitable linearization of the DOM trees has to be found. For this task we use several strategies of tree node traversal: Pre-Order, Post-Order and Breath-First-Search (BFS) traversal. Figure (1) shows a linearization of two sample trees using Post-Order and how the resulting sequences S_{T_i} may have been aligned for the best alignment distance. We have enhanced the labels of the linearized nodes by adding the in- and out degrees corresponding to the former position of the nodes in the tree. This information can be used during the computation of the alignment cost: An example of this is that the alignment of two nodes with identical HTML-tags but different in/out degrees will result in a higher cost than in cases where these degrees match. Following this strategy, at least part of the structure information is preserved. This approach is followed by Dehmer (2005) who develops a special form of tree linearization which is based on tree levels.

Obviously, a linearization poses a loss of structure information which has impact on the results of distance measurement. But the computational complexity of sequence alignments ($O(n^2)$) is significantly better than of tree edit distances. This leads to a trade-off between the expressiveness of the DOM-Tree representation (in our case tree vs. linearization to a sequence) and the complexity of the algorithms to compute the distance thereon. In order to have a baseline for tree linearization techniques we have also tested random linearizations. According to this method, trees are transformed into sequences of nodes in random order. For our experiment we have generated 16 random linearizations and computed the median of their categorization performances.

Next, we perform pairwise distance measurements of the DOM-trees using the set of algorithms described above. We then apply two clustering methods on the resulting distance matrices: hierarchical agglomerative and k-means clustering. Hierarchical agglomerative clustering does not need any information on the expected number of clusters so we examine all possible clusterings and chose the one maximizing the F-measure. However we also examine how well hierarchical clustering performs if the number of partitions is restricted to the number of categories. In contrast to the previous approach, k-means needs to be informed about the number of clusters in advance, which in the present experiment equals the number of categories, which in our case is four. Because we know the category of each article we can perform an exhaustive parameter study to maximize the well known efficiency measures *purity*, *inverse purity* and the combined *F-measure*.

3.4 Results and discussion

The tables (3) and (5) show the results for corpus variant I (using all HTML-tags) and variant II (using structure relevant HTML-tags only) (see section 3.2). The general picture is that hierarchical clustering performs significantly better than k-means. However this is only the case for an unrestricted number of clusters. If we restrict the number of clusters for hierarchical clustering to the number of categories, the differences become much less apparent (see tables 4 and 6). The only exception to this is marked by the tree edit distance: The best F-measure of 0.863 is achieved by using 58 clusters. If we restrict the number of clusters to 4, tree edit still reaches an F-measure of 0.710 which is significantly higher than the best k-means result of 0.599.

As one would intuitively expect the results achieved by the tree edit distance are much better than the variants of tree linearization. The edit distance operates on trees whereas the other algorithms are bound to less informative sequences. Interestingly, the differences become much less apparent for the corpus variant II which consists of the simplified DOM-trees (see section 3.2). We can assume that the advantage of the tree edit distance over the linearization-based approaches diminishes, the smaller the trees to be compared are.

The performance of the different variants of tree linearization vary only significantly in the case of unrestricted hierarchical clustering (see tables 3 and 5). In the case of k-means as well as in the case of restricting hierarchical clustering to exactly 4 clusters, the performances are about equal.

In order to provide a baseline for better rating the cluster results, we perform random clustering. This leads to an F-measure of 0.311 (averaged over 1,000 runs). Content-based categorization experiments using the bag of words model have reported F-measures of about 0.86 (Yang, 1999).

The baseline for the different variants of lin-

Similarity Algorithm	Clustering Algorithm	# Clusters	F-Measure	Purity	Inverse Purity	PW Distance	Method-Specifical
tree edit distance	hierarchical	58	0.863	0.996	0.786	none	weighted linkage
post-order linearization	hierarchical	13	0.775	0.809	0.775	spearman	single linkage
pre-order linearization	hierarchical	19	0.741	0.817	0.706	spearman	single linkage
tree level linearization	hierarchical	36	0.702	0.882	0.603	spearman	single linkage
bfs linearization	hierarchical	13	0.696	0.698	0.786	spearman	single linkage
tree edit distance	k-means	4	0.599	0.618	0.641	-	cosine distance
pre-order linearization	k-means	4	0.595	0.615	0.649	-	cosine distance
post-order linearization	k-means	4	0.593	0.615	0.656	-	cosine distance
tree level linearization	k-means	4	0.593	0.603	0.649	-	cosine distance
random lin. (medians only)	-	-	0.591	0.563	0.795	-	-
bfs linearization	k-means	4	0.580	0.595	0.656	-	cosine distance
-	random	4	0.311	0.362	0.312	-	-

Table 3: Evaluation results using all tags.

Similarity Algorithm	Clustering Algorithm	# Clusters	F-Measure	Purity	Inverse Purity	PW Distance	Method-Specifical
tree edit distance	hierarchical	4	0.710	0.698	0.851	spearman	single linkage
bfs linearization	hierarchical	4	0.599	0.565	0.851	none	weighted linkage
tree level linearization	hierarchical	4	0.597	0.615	0.676	spearman	complete linkage
post-order linearization	hierarchical	4	0.595	0.615	0.683	spearman	average linkage
pre-order linearization	hierarchical	4	0.578	0.599	0.660	cosine	average linkage

Table 4: Evaluation results using all tags and hierarchical clustering with a fixed number of clusters.

earization is given by random linearizations: We perform 16 random linearizations, run the different variants of distance measurement as well as clustering and compute the median of the best F-measure values achieved. These are 0.591 for corpus variant I and 0.581 for the simplified variant II. These results are in fact surprising because they are only little worse than the other linearization techniques. This result may indicate that – in the present scenario – the linearization based approaches to tree distance measurement are not suitable because of the loss of structure information. More specifically, this raises the following antithesis: Either, the sequence-oriented models of measuring structural similarities taken into account are insensitive to the structuring of web documents. Or: this structuring only counts what regards the degrees of nodes and their labels irrespective of their order. As tree-oriented methods perform better, we view this to be an argument against linearization oriented methods, at least what regards the present evaluation scenario *to which only DOM trees are input* but not more general graph structures.

The experiment has shown that analyzing the document structure provides a remarkable amount of information to categorization. It also shows that the sensitivity of the approaches used in different contexts needs to be further explored which we will address in our future research.

4 Conclusion

We presented a cluster-based approach to structure learning in the area of web documents. This was done in order to approach the goal of a combined algorithm of webgenre exploration *and* categorization. As argued in section (1), such an algorithm is needed in web corpus linguistics for webgenre tagging as a prerequisite of measuring genre-sensitive collocations. In order to evaluate the present approach, we utilized a corpus of wiki-based articles. The evaluation showed that there is an information gain when measuring the similarities of web documents irrespective of their lexical content. This is in the line of the genre model of systemic functional linguistics (Ventola, 1987) which prospects an impact of genre membership on text structure. As the corpus used for evaluation is limited to tree-like structures, this approach is in need for further development. Future work will address this task. This regards especially the classification of graph-like representations of web documents which take their link structure into account.

References

Einat Amitay, David Carmel, Adam Darlow, Ronny Lempel, and Aya Soffer. 2003. The connectivity sonar: detecting site functionality by structural patterns. In *Proc. of the 14th ACM conference on Hypertext and Hypermedia*, pages 38–47.

Marco Baroni and Silvia Bernardini, editors. 2006. *WaCky! Working papers on the Web as corpus.* Gedit, Bologna, Italy.

Philip Bille. 2003. Tree edit distance, alignment distance and inclusion. Technical report TR-2003-23.

Soumen Chakrabarti, Byron Dom, and Piotr Indyk.

Similarity Algorithm	Clustering Algorithm	# Clusters	F-Measure	Purity	Inverse Purity	PW Distance	Method-Specifical
tree edit distance	hierarchical	51	0.756	0.905	0.691	none	weighted linkage
pre-order linearization	hierarchical	20	0.742	0.809	0.771	spearman	single linkage
post-order linearization	hierarchical	23	0.732	0.813	0.756	spearman	single linkage
tree level linearization	hierarchical	2	0.607	0.553	0.878	spearman	weighted linkage
bfs linearization	hierarchical	4	0.589	0.603	0.641	cosine	weighted linkage
tree edit distance	k-means	4	0.713	0.718	0.718	-	cosine distance
pre-order linearization	k-means	4	0.587	0.603	0.634	-	cosine distance
tree level linearization	k-means	4	0.584	0.603	0.641	-	cosine distance
bfs linearization	k-means	4	0.583	0.599	0.637	-	cosine distance
post-order linearization	k-means	4	0.582	0.592	0.630	-	cosine distance
random lin. (medians only)	-	-	0.581	0.584	0.674	-	-
-	random	4	0.311	0.362	0.312	-	-

Table 5: Evaluation results using structure relevant tags only.

Similarity Algorithm	Clustering Algorithm	# Clusters	F-Measure	Purity	Inverse Purity	PW Distance	Method-Specifical
tree edit distance	hierarchical	4	0.643	0.645	0.793	spearman	average linkage
post-order linearization	hierarchical	4	0.629	0.634	0.664	spearman	average linkage
tree level linearization	hierarchical	4	0.607	0.595	0.679	spearman	weighted linkage
bfs linearization	hierarchical	4	0.589	0.603	0.641	cosine	weighted linkage
pre-order linearization	hierarchical	4	0.586	0.603	0.660	cosine	complete linkage

Table 6: Evaluation results using all tags and hierarchical clustering with a fixed number of clusters.

1998. Enhanced hypertext categorization using hyperlinks. In *Proceedings of ACM SIGMOD International Conference on Management of Data*, pages 307–318. ACM.

Weimin Chen. 2001. New algorithm for ordered tree-to-tree correction problem. *Journal of Algorithms*, 40(2):135–158.

Matthias Dehmer. 2005. *Strukturelle Analyse Web-basierter Dokumente*. Ph.D. thesis, Technische Universität Darmstadt, Fachbereich Informatik.

Johannes Fürnkranz. 1999. Exploiting structural information for text classification on the WWW. In *Proceedings of the Third International Symposium on Advances in Intelligent Data Analysis*, pages 487–498, Berlin/New York. Springer.

M. Höchsmann, T. Töller, R. Giegerich, and S. Kurtz. 2003. Local similarity in rna secondary structures. In *Proc. Computational Systems Bioinformatics*, pages 159–168.

Chih-Wei Hsu, Chih-Chung Chang, and Chih-Jen Lin. 2003. A practical guide to SVM classification. Technical report, Department of Computer Science and Information Technology, National Taiwan University.

Thorsten Joachims. 2002. *Learning to classify text using support vector machines*. Kluwer, Boston.

Adam Kilgarriff and Gregory Grefenstette. 2003. Introduction to the special issue on the web as corpus. *Computational Linguistics*, 29(3):333–347.

P. Klein. 1998. Computing the edit-distance between unrooted ordered trees. In G. Bilardi, G. F. Italiano, A. Pietracaprina, and G. Pucci, editors, *Proceedings of the 6th Annual European Symposium*, pages 91–102, Berlin. Springer.

Jon M. Kleinberg. 1999. Authoritative sources in a hyperlinked environment. *Journal of the ACM*, 46(5):604–632.

Alexander Mehler and Rüdiger Gleim. 2005. The net for the graphs — towards webgenre representation for corpus linguistic studies. In Marco Baroni and Silvia Bernardini, editors, *WaCky! Working papers on the Web as corpus*. Gedit, Bologna, Italy.

Alexander Mehler, Rüdiger Gleim, and Matthias Dehmer. 2005. Towards structure-sensitive hypertext categorization. In *Proceedings of the 29th Annual Conference of the German Classification Society*, Berlin. Springer.

Yoshiaki Mizuuchi and Keishi Tajima. 1999. Finding context paths for web pages. In *Proceedings of the 10th ACM Conference on Hypertext and Hypermedia*, pages 13–22.

Michael Stubbs. 2001. On inference theories and code theories: Corpus evidence for semantic schemas. *Text*, 21(3):437–465.

K. C. Tai. 1979. The tree-to-tree correction problem. *Journal of the ACM*, 26(3):422–433.

Eija Ventola. 1987. *The Structure of Social Interaction: a Systemic Approach to the Semiotics of Service Encounters*. Pinter, London.

Yiming Yang, Sean Slattery, and Rayid Ghani. 2002. A study of approaches to hypertext categorization. *Journal of Intelligent Information Systems*, 18(2-3):219–241.

Yiming Yang. 1999. An evaluation of statistical approaches to text categorization. *Journal of Information Retrieval*, 1(1/2):67–88.

K. Zhang and D. Shasha. 1989. Simple fast algorithms for the editing distance between trees and related problems. *SIAM Journal of Computing*, 18:1245–1262.